ASKING THE NEXT QUESTION

Leonard Kaplan
Wayne State University

College Town Press
P.O. Box 669, Bloomington, Indiana 47402

To Evelyn

To Brian, Sheri and Donna

and to our newest arrival
Scott Ryan

May you grow up and possess the same level of affect
as your grandmother, parents and aunt.

College Town Press books are printed in the United States of America by Tichenor Publishing Group, a division of T.I.S. Enterprises.

Copyright © 1986 by College Town Press
All Rights Reserved

ISBN 0-89917-474-4

No part of this publication may be reproduced by any means whatsoever without the prior written permission of the copyright owner. For information, write College Town Press, A Division of T.I.S. Enterprises, P.O. Box 669, Bloomington, IN 47402.

Table of Contents

Introduction v

Chapter One: Some Thoughts About Cognition 1
    Higher Level Thinking Skills 2
    Sample Taxonomy Questions 5
    Summary 6
    Review 6

Chapter Two: The Affective Domain 9
    What is it? 9
    The Affective Continuum 11
    Summary 14
    Review 14

Chapter Three: A Systematic Approach to Classroom Analysis 17
    Teaching 17
    Objective #1—Studying Children 18
    Objective #2—Studying Instruction 20
    Objective #3—Studying One's Self 22
    Summary 24
    Review 25

Chapter Four: The Taxonomy of Affective Behavior (T.A.B.) 29
    Mechanics for Recording Data 30
    Summary 43
    Review 45

Chapter Five: Curriculum Activities 49
    Section One—Lesson Plans 49
    Section Two—More Lesson Plans (But with a Difference) 56

Chapter Six: Be Creative 67

Chapter Seven: Summary 87

Appendix A: The Taxonomy of Affective Behavior in the Classroom 91
Appendix B: The Date 95

Answers to Review Sections 99

Bibliography 105

Introduction

In 1978 my book, *Developing Objectives In the Affective Domain* was published. Reactions to it have been interesting. I've received feed-back ranging from "complicated, confusing and very technical," to, "simplistic, ambitious and sounds easy." Of course these judgments tend to be at the extremes and not necessarily reflective of the majority of readers. There have been those who have used superlatives to describe this text but since these careful and discriminating individuals represent my family, friends and students their motives and biases could be suspect. However, I gratefully accept affect from those who wish to provide it.

The majority of readers seem to be made up of people who have classroom responsibilities in need of assistance. These teachers work with children in school, adults in the workplace, parents in the home and students in college. Some of these individuals hold teaching certificates; many do not. What they have in common is their need to develop experiences for their students that are cognitively significant as well as personally relevant. It is to this population that this book is directed.

It seems apparent, at least to this observer, that many teachers, at all levels, have difficulty asking provocative questions that trigger more than one word responses. Questions such as, "who did what when," or "what is the correct answer," seem to be the way of many classrooms. This line of questioning relies totally on memorization or recall for the "right" answer. How the student arrived at point B from point A seems insignificant in the fact of being at point B. In other words, if the learner is at the desired place why press your luck. Just thank whomever you wish to thank and keep moving.

Assuming that we are interested in our students internalizing this material, suggesting that they can process its meaning, then it becomes obvious that other questions need asking. Not only do we need to ask "why," we may also want to ask, "who cares" or "what difference does it make?" These are the questions that promote the highest intellectual payoffs.

It is this probing that separates classes or learners. To memorize and then respond at call is one thing. To be able to make some sense out of these data and then process it for use whenever needed is what this teacher desires. To do this will require *"Asking The Next Question."*

This book has a point of view; it is that affect, or the expression of feelings, attitudes and values should not be incidental in the classroom. The opportunity of providing learners with the skills necessary to develop attitudes consistent with a system of beliefs is fundamental if educators are to come close to achieving some of the cardinal principles talked about for years. The argument, whether academic education as opposed to progressive education playing a major role in the preparation of young people, seems to be a never ending debate. Why these philosophical points of view seem to be incompatible leaves one to wonder. However, the debate continues. As a school tax millage election arrives proponents from each camp present themselves to campaign for or against the teaching of human values through the humanities. Concerns are expressed to reinstate the instructional programs in art, music, literature, nature and "life-long" commitments. Quick to respond are those who deplore crime in the streets, unusually high unemployment of young people, attributing these problems to the failure of school to provide the "basics" to its students. "Forget the frills, get back to teaching the fundamentals of reading, writing and arithmetic." "Above all, stress discipline."

One definition for the word freedom is that a free person has alternatives. A free person can make choices; choices on where to live and how to live. The promise of education is that it should and can provide its consumers with the skills that will assist in the opportunity to gain these alternatives. Certainly the acquisition of basic skills in the 3 R's is fundamental to this end. Equally fundamental are the humanities which will help shape the attitudes and perceptions of our youth. It has even been suggested that it is through the humanities that a learner can truly implement the knowledges acquired from the academics.

This book is for those who teach or desire to teach. It is designed in such a way as to provide the educator the opportunity of using the ideas, goals and objectives discussed here in building curriculum for the classroom. It is the desire of the author that this book be viewed as a "how to" rather than a totally theoretical work which, with much study and time, may be practical to the classroom teacher. This may be an overly ambitious goal; however, it is the goal. It is hoped that there will be sufficient ideas generated either in the book or by the book to assist the user in bringing together the arts and sciences for the purpose of achieving a higher priority; that is, the identification of a system of beliefs, values and attitudes that permits the learner to use knowledge and skill in a way that will permit him/her to be able to make choices or to seek alternatives. Information for information sake is limiting. Art for art's sake is frustrating. It is the role of the teacher to bring these together, through a meaningful curriculum, so that the learner can make some sense out of it all.

Chapter One is about cognition. Its intent is to provide the reader with some definitions of what this word means and how it can be classified into various levels. It is important that we know this so that we can begin to fuse this domain with that of affect. The strong bias contained within this manuscript is that affect stimulates higher levels of cognitive thought. Affective behavior is not an end product unto itself. It is a mechanism that deals with self actualization and also provides a vehicle for more productive thinking.

Chapter Two attempts to define affective behavior as it will be used in this manuscript. Some discussion and examples will be provided in an effort to illustrate what it is we are trying to identify and measure. At the end of each chapter some questions will be asked to assure your understanding of the material. If you have any difficulty it is suggested that you might wish to reread that portion of the book that is causing the problem. Answers to these questions are provided in the back of the book.

Chapter Three discusses the rationale for and the building of an observational system. It is through such a system that the teacher can identify what it is he/she wishes to teach and thus provide feed-back as to whether or not what was hopefully taught was actually learned.

Chapter Four provides the reader with a description of the Taxonomy of Affective Behavior in the Classroom (T.A.B.). This instrument provides forty-five (45) objectives or behaviors in the affective domain which can be used by the teacher in the development of curriculum. The reader will discover how the Taxonomy works as a feed-back instrument in addition to its uses as a vehicle that stimulates the affective behaviors of learners. Each of the behaviors contained within the T.A.B. will be described. By defining and providing examples of each behavior the reader is able to see how each objective can achieve curriculum outcomes. Examples will be provided for all levels of the educational spectrum.

The intent of the Fifth Chapter is to provide a hands-on opportunity for the reader. Mini-lessons are available as exercises to assure that you understand what objectives are being developed. This will assure that the reader comprehends a) how the T.A.B. is used, b) how curriculum can be developed and, c) provides the reader immediate feed-back regarding a level of understanding of the definitions of each of the objectives listed in the instrument. You are encouraged to write in the book as you would in any exercise material. Answer sheets are available in the back of the book to check accuracy and comprehension.

In Chapter Six, the reader is encouraged to develop his/her own lesson plans or activities using the photographs and topical suggestions as a stimulus. Hopefully the practice provided in the preceeding chapter will facilitate this experience.

Chapter Seven is a summary of the material covered or hopefully uncovered in this book.

Enough! Now let's get on with it.

Chapter One

SOME THOUGHTS ABOUT COGNITION

A few years ago a second grader wrote an essay dealing with the purpose of education. Her paper read: "The purpose of second grade is to get into third grade." This view of education might, in a nutshell, capture the belief that schooling is a series of hurdles each to be jumped on the way to another. The end of the race comes with the awarding of the medals or ribbons to the winners. It seems that the purpose of grade twelve is to finish it. Those who complete the task graduate. There are those in our society who question what graduation means. What does it signify in terms of accomplishment? What's been won or lost?

A number of studies, quite respectable for their soundness of design, have indicated that the pattern of instruction most common in our classrooms is that which asks the student to recall a piece of information. Teachers normally ask their students to either read, listen or look at something. Typically the student either reads from some text, listens to a lecture or views something from a screen (computer, film, T.V.). The student or class is then asked to respond to a series of questions that will, hopefully, bring the learner to the place of acquisition. With all due respect to Professor Kingsfield and Socrates, questions that probe beyond basic facts are just not all that common. Of course, we have known for a long time that internalization can only take place when we arrive at the point of higher level thinking skills.

Bloom and associates have pointed out that acquiring knowledge is at the lowest level of the cognitive spectrum. Gaining specific information is important especially if the game of school demands it. Doing well on the Scholastic Aptitude Test (S.A.T.'s) or in the game *Trivial Pursuit* have taken on new and important meanings to both parents and educators. Academic excellence seems to be measured through the multiple choice, fill in the blank or true, false response. Of course our willingness to permit these measures to dictate competence clearly directs a curriculum as well as adds undue pressures to school people and most especially students. And yet, this demand for facts is continually emphasized knowing that this level, while important, is at the bottom of the taxonomy.

Demographers and futurists indicate that major employment opportunities will be available in the service industries. Those who occupy these positions will be expected to be knowledgeable in their subject. However, if these individuals are to help others it is expected that they will also possess the skills to interpret data, translate this information in a meaningful way so that others may effectively analyze the circumstances and then make appropriate decisions. Having a genuine interest in people and attending to their needs will also be required. Caring about the individual being served hopefully will regain some importance in our society. In a world seemingly committed to worshipping microchips, a renewed commitment to affective variables may be welcomed. Attention to affect will need at least equal billing if students are to develop expertise and transfer these attitudinal skills into observable behaviors. More about this in a later chapter.

HIGHER LEVEL THINKING SKILLS

Since it is the intent of this book to speak directly to the practitioner, it seems appropriate to attempt to identify those areas that students will need some assistance in developing. The descriptions that follow are those cognitive categories articulated by Bloom et al. (with slight variation). An attempt will be made to try to describe them as they pertain to the classroom setting. Definitions will be given in a way as to describe what they may be like in our daily teaching practice. What are the next questions?

Memory

This has been mentioned. Memorization and recall skills are demanded from our learners. This writer has no quarrel with the teacher who asks students to repeat what has been said elsewhere. Certainly not all knowledge is new. Major discoveries have come about because new knowledge was placed above what is already known. To be able to remember and use what others have seen or thought about makes sense. However, rediscovering the wheel though popular and sometimes productive, is overdone.

Translation

In an effort to develop understanding it is often necessary to rephrase or describe words or events. Those who translate from one language to another do this all the time. It is clear in this example that an individual may have the tools to understand and thereby process the material, however this individual may not have the facility of language. A phrase often used is, "It's Greek to me." This of course is used when we have heard the words, read the material or viewed the data but still lack understanding. The problem may not be in the words themselves but a lack of understanding regarding their meaning. One way to ascertain meaning, from a teacher's view, is to have the student do the translating. The teacher may frequently ask the learner to identify something. That is a memory or recall type question. Determining a student's ability to translate will require asking the next question. This question might be to describe the activity. Asking the learner to paraphrase the material might be the way to go. To be sure, this does not guarantee understanding but it does suggest that the learner can do more than just repeat something. It does take more savvy to translate than just recall. The next question had to be asked.

Interpretation

The ability to interpret suggests some level of understanding. Dancers interpret a story or a feeling by performing it. Their movements suggest a visual comprehension of what the author or composer had intended. A musician studies the composer and attempts to identify with his feelings at the time the piece was composed. The music that comes out suggests how one individual hears and views another.

In our classrooms we interpret material by being able to compare it to other works, identifying similarities and/or differences that exist between it and other works. Hopefully, it is obvious that this level of cognition can not be achieved unless questions or experiences are provided for the learner that specifically focus in at this level.

Application

At this level the learner must provide visible evidence to support the position that learning has occurred. Just listening to a response is not enough to substantiate this level of internalization. The ability to apply suggests the skill of using information in situational contexts. We expect information to apply to experiences other than the one directly at hand. The learner should be required to apply previous learning to new situations.

The student should be able to create as well as solve problems. The facility to create something demonstrates the student's depth of understanding regarding how one or more things fit into other contexts and surroundings. Clearly the student can identify the who, what, where and when. At this level it is also expected that the students can explain or demonstrate the how and why. We may need to ask a few next questions to arrive at this point.

Analysis

This area promotes the idea that evidence is expected in the defense of a position. Those who have taught have learned that many students have strong feelings unsupported by any reasonable form of documentation. Upon further reflection this may be true for many adults. Strong emotion does not necessarily equate to valid argument. Analytical behavior demands a why or a rationale. It further demands reasons for feelings. Asking questions that get to the root is imperative in this intellectual process. Acceptance of the first response rarely gets to this depth. The "right" answer does not provide causality. The key to working in this area is the word evidence. It is expected that the learner will provide data to support conclusions and further more this data will be well organized and logical.

Synthesis

The ability to function at this level takes some doing and most important, some understanding. Learners who perform here are able to elaborate on material. They can expand on meaning since they are able to pull from various sources to make their position or content more clear. Since it is clear that learners who can synthesize can put together pieces of things or ideas we often see these individuals proposing a plan or rule for proceeding in endeavors. Students who can synthesize may become effective actors since they can piece together items and create their own stories or plays. Teachers who describe students functioning at this level may be challenged to provide a variety of stimuli from which the learner may draw conclusions. Just having the basal reader or basic text available may not be enough. Importance is placed on testing or examining many ideas, many materials, many philosophies and theories. We may have to examine a variety of hymnals rather than just one. There will be many next questions examined here.

Evaluation

Last but far from insignificant. Leaders in business and industry looking for future employees are clear in their demand for personnel who can gather data, examine this information and make appropriate decisions based on identifiable criteria, rules or plans. In other words, folks who can think through a problem and effectively deal with it. Creative decision makers have learned to operate at all levels identified in the hierarchy. Teachers will be expected to provide opportunities for learners to acquire these process skills. They can be taught. They are not learned through osmosis but rather by experience in their operations. It should be clear that instructors considered effective will build into their curricular design opportunities for these occurrences. Our society demands graduates from the schools who are employably marketable. Marketability means knowing how to operate at these levels.

SAMPLE TAXONOMY QUESTIONS*

"Goldilocks"

1. **Knowledge**

   What things did Goldilocks do in the three bears' house?

2. **Translation**

   Why did Goldilocks try all the furniture in the three bears' house?

3. **Interpretation**

   Why did she like the baby bear's things best?

4. **Application**

   If Goldilocks came to your house, what things would she do?

5. **Analysis**

   What things in the story could really have happened?

6. **Synthesis**

   Retell the story as it would be if it were called, "Goldilocks and the Three Fishes."

7. **Evaluation**

   Do you think that it was right for Goldilocks to go into the three bears' house without being invited? Why or why not?

*Author Unkown

SUMMARY

Knowledge for knowledge sake has its benefits. It permits the possesser of this information to do well when called upon to recite what he can recall. As our society puts increasing demands on the school it will be necessary to require teachers to know more and for learners to know more. These demands are not always unreasonable. A complicated and absorbing society expects each generation to know more than the one before it. It assumes that those involved with instruction will know more, be better prepared and be up on the latest in technology.

However, as some things change others remain constant. Each generation, hopefully, has demanded that its learner be prepared to do more than memorize information and provide feed-back on standardized tests. Of course this may be wishful thinking since our apparent goal has been to raise S.A.T. scores. Each of us has been called upon to bring meaning to our learning; to provide insight that goes beyond the regurgitation of acquired knowledge. In other words, we've been asked to think. Sometimes even critically.

The purpose behind this chapter was to identify the cognitive areas that go beyond the lowest level of the Bloom's Taxonomy and suggest that those of us involved in developing teaching/learning strategies can assist students in their critical thinking by asking questions that stimulate these higher levels.

REVIEW OF CHAPTER ONE

1. Define "higher level thinking skills."

2. List the seven general categories contained within the cognitive hierarchy in order from simple to complex.

   a.

   b.

   c.

   d.

   e.

   f.

   g.

3. Define each of the seven levels of cognition.

   a.

   b.

   c.

   d.

   e.

   f.

   g.

Chapter Two

THE AFFECTIVE DOMAIN

WHAT IS IT?

A principal I know in describing a teacher became extremely flowery in her use of superlatives. This teacher is in the judgment of this school administrator, *"sensitive* to the needs of youngsters, *understanding* of their problems and unusually *empathetic* to their needs." In addition, "his sense of *fairness* is only exceeded by his keen sense of *humor* and his untiring *enthusiasm* for teaching and learning." High praise, indeed. In fact, it's so good we should try to bottle what it is the teacher is doing so that all teachers can behave in a like manner. However, as we all know, things are not that simple. Each of us would agree that it is desirable for all teachers to possess characteristics that will not only endear us to our learners, but above all facilitate learning. Unfortunately the old saying is true; "love is in the eye of the beholder." What is seen as sensitivity in one person is perceived as weakness in another. Sense of humor can also take the form of sarcasm or ridicule.

As a generalization, the affective domain may be said to consist of such factors as emotions, values, attitudes, appreciations, impressions, desires, feelings, preferences, interests, temperament, integrity, character, love-of-beauty, aesthetics, and the like. Clearly, these are vague terms. They are vague in the sense they convey different meanings to different persons. This ambiguity in terminology is part of the problem encountered in discussing the affective domain.

The affective domain is huge and it is complex. Being huge and complex, and in the absence of a standard terminology, is it any wonder that you and I, as teachers, are placed at a severe disadvantage in the endeavor to formulate such objectives, plan educational experiences around these and finally, assess how well our students attain them? Objectives that are vague and unclear have a way of becoming haphazard, poorly planned and less than adequate learning experiences for our children. In fact, most of us, when pushed, will admit that while we are trying to provide for the feelings, emotions, and sensitivities of children, we are less than satisfied about the success of our efforts.

The affective domain contrasts sharply with the cognitive in that the cognitive has to do primarily with growth and development of *intellectual* skills and abilities. Although it is an oversimplification, it may be said that the cognitive has to do with the mind, *with thinking,* while the affective has to do with the emotions, *with feeling.* This is not to say that the two domains do not overlap, because they do. In fact, in some respects, it is almost impossible to distinguish between the two.

The affective domain is significant in its own right. It is of tremendous concern to all of us as teachers at all levels from kindergarten through graduate school. However, despite this almost universal concern of faculty, the affective domain tends to be severely slighted in the everyday-ongoing emphasis on reading, writing and arithmetic. It is slighted too at the administrative levels and by school boards of education. We see this reflected in the emphasis on reading and arithmetic in comparison with the minimal or even non-existent emphasis on music and art. We see it indirectly in our reluctance as a people to allow or even encourage feelings to come forth and be shared. Aesthetics are still afterthoughts "if there is time and money left after the essentials." Harry Broudy put it quite well when he asked "What's basic in Basic Education?"[1]

Reasons for the relatively limited emphasis on the affective areas in contrast to the cognitive are not difficult to locate. For one thing, there is the scarcity of really significant research on the growth stages of the affective domain. For another, there is the limited amount of research on the nature of the relationships between the cognitive and the affective domains. Earlier, it was suggested that there is an absence of a standard terminology. Add to this the lack of valid, standardized instruments such as tests, scales, inventories and observational devices in affective areas.

Also of considerable importance in contributing to the limited attention given to the affective areas of child development is the cultural reluctance in the United States to evaluate students along these lines. In our culture, for example, it is felt that a person's beliefs, values, attitudes and feelings are private. These are 'his business' and his alone and are not to be pried into or 'meddled' with in any way. This attitude of ours contrasts sharply with our contrary cultural orientation to the effect that a person's *cognitive achievement* is of public interest. That a person's achievement is, rightfully, to be made known to the public is evidenced by our publishing of names on the honor roll, announcement in the newspaper of the receipt of scholarships, open comparison of student report cards, parental attempts to accelerate children in

---

[1] Paper presented at the National Symposium on Teaching and Learning, sponsored by the College of Education, University of Illinois, October, 1977.

school, our vocalizing about the students who are smart versus those who are dumb, etc. Achievement, both cognitive and physical, receive wide acclaim, as does achievement in vocations which require mental competence. But we are concerned that involvement with the affective area moves us rather close to what might be termed indoctrination and that, indeed, is shaky ground for us to tread upon in a democracy. Kohlberg best describes this point when he discusses the difference between teaching moral development rather than values.[2]

Still another factor contributing to our reluctance to proceed in school with the affective domain is the difficulty of attributing specific changes in our students to the specific activities of particular teachers. How does any teacher really know that Johnny's frequent browsing in the town library stems from her work with him in reading? Does Sally's interest in bird watching result from a class discussion in science? To what extent does even a portion of a student's interest in a hobby derive from the efforts of a particular teacher? Indeed, wherein does the influence of the home enter into and supercede the influence of the school? Or, in what respects do the influences of the home and school interact in contributing to the attainment or lack of attainment of certain objectives?

In the past decade, teachers at all levels have demonstrated that they can construct and use quality objectives in the cognitive domain. In fact, monies have been provided at the federal, state and local levels for this purpose. Hopefully teachers will become equally proficient in constructing and using objectives in the affective domain.

THE AFFECTIVE CONTINUUM

The affective domain can be arranged in a hierarchy proceeding along a continuum from the very simple to the very complex. Each level rests upon the preceding lower level. Therefore, as one moves along the continuum, each specific objective becomes a subset of the larger or more complex objective which follows. This arrangement clearly suggests that facts or information giving is important. However, this information is only significant as it relates to ideas, concepts and educational constructs. Chapter Three will deal with this hierarchy in some detail, outlining an affective hierarchy or taxonomy and giving specific definitions and examples for each behavior listed.

However, to follow through on what is being presented here you need to know the general categories.[3]

---

[2]Lawrence Kohlberg, *Stages of Moral Development as a Basis for Moral Education* (New York: Beck, Crittendon and Sullivan, 1976).

[3]Krathwohl *et al.*

1. **Receiving (Attending)**

   At this level the learner is sensitive to the existence of certain phenomena and stimuli. The learner is willing to receive or attend to them. The learner is not actively committed to acceptance or rejection of the phenomena into his personal value system.

   1.1 Awareness

   This category is concerned with the knowledge of something through alertness in observing or interpreting what one sees, hears, feels, etc. It does not imply an assessment of the qualities or nature of the stimulus. It suggests simple awareness without specific characteristics having an effect.

   1.2 Willingness to Receive

   Ability to tolerate a given stimulus, not to avoid it. This involves a neutrality or suspended judgment toward the stimulus. Given the opportunity to attend in a field with relatively few competing stimuli, the learner is not actively seeking to avoid it. At best, he is willing to take notice of the phenomenon and give it his attention.

2. **Responding**

   Responses in this category go beyond merely attending or alertness to the stimulus. The person is committing himself, at a very low level, to the phenomenon involved. The "value" is not yet his, although he is doing something with or about the phenomenon besides merely perceiving it.

3. **Valuing**

   This category is concerned with the amount of worth that an individual places on a value. At the lowest level he may be only estimating the worth of the value and at the highest level he shows definite commitment to the value and actively incorporates the idea into his intrinsic system. At this level his behavior is affected by the value.

   3.1 Preference for a Value

   The person selects from alternative values. He may either accept or reject the value. A degree of commitment is involved in his acceptance or rejection.

4. **Organization**

   This category describes the beginnings of the building of a value system. Concepts of values are highly abstract. Individual behavior which denotes the value can be observed and compared to a norm as defined by the individual, teacher, society, school or class, etc. For example, a specific individual school may value cleanliness. The degree to which an individual student in the school values cleanliness can be observed against the background of the other students in the school. That is, the student's cleanliness is either less than, more than, or the same as the average student.

5. **Characterization by a Value or Value Complex**

   At this level of internalization the values already have a place in the individual's value hierarchy, are organized into some kind of internally consistent system, have controlled the behavior of the individual for a sufficient time that he has adapted to behaving this way; to call forth the behavior no longer arouses emotion except when the individual is threatened or challenged.

   5.1 Generalized Set

   This category is concerned with the person's basic orientation which enables him to reduce and order the complex world about him and to act consistently and effectively in it.

   5.2 Characterization

   The behavior describes the personality.

As seen by this listing the continuum involves the ordering of phenomena from the simplest situation of a child being barely aware of any stimuli to that ultimate situation at which time the child or adult can be described as having internalized a value or belief as part of his philosophy of life. For example, at the beginning of the learner's awareness he sees that there is an interdependence among and between his peers. Initially this is merely perceived. At the opposite end of the continuum the person might evaluate the actions of

---

[4]The reader is advised to see Appendix B for a listing of the categories contained with Bloom's Cognitive Domain.

his peers in terms of issues rather than on his own biases or ethnocentricism. Stated in an objective format, these goals might appear as follows:

1. Student is aware that the actions of one person may affect other individuals.

2. The student concludes that injustices committed by his peers are unwarranted and should not be tolerated.

SUMMARY

The purpose behind this chapter is relatively obvious. It is that the affective domain can be identified and therefore defined. It has become too apparent that many teachers treat this vital area quite casually out of either a lack of understanding of what affect is, or the belief that the acquisition of cognitive skills is the primary responsibility of the learner and therefore the top agenda item for the teacher.

The affective domain can be looked upon as a hierarchy of activities. That is, items that would be classified in this area can be treated as relatively simple to quite complex. As in the case of many disciplines it is necessary to know some basic skills or basic understandings since more complex skills and understandings are built upon this knowledge. In the continuum presented in this chapter it was pointed out that there are five general categories that make up this domain. These categories attempt to classify the variety of behaviors or objectives that fall within its boundaries and lay the foundation for considering some curriculum issues that will be discussed in later chapters.

REVIEW OF CHAPTER TWO

1. List five factors that comprise the affective domain.

   a. _____

   b. _____

   c. _____

   d. _____

   e. _____

2. The cognitive domain has to do primarily with (a.) _____

   _____ while the affective domain has to

   do with (b.) _____ .

3. List three reasons why the affective domain seems to be overlooked in our classrooms.

   a. _____

   b. _____

   c. _____

4. List the five general categories contained within the affective hierarchy in order from very simple to very complex.

   a. _____

   b. _____

   c. _____

   d. _____

   e. _____

5. Select the item that would best fit under Category 1 of the affective continuum.

   a–1. Sue will be able to type 30 words a minute at the end of the semester.
   2. Herman can recite Lincoln's Gettysburg Address without any notes or coaching.
   3. Mary is aware that Ralph is crying.
   4. Willie can add 3 columns of numbers with an 80% degree of accuracy.

b- 1. All of the students in the music class can play the scales on the piano.
   2. Dr. Rappoport can perform a medical task without sending a bill.
   3. Waldo can run 100 yards in less than 12 seconds.
   4. The school principal will be able to recognize his own bias as bias.

6. Select the item that would best fit under Category 2 of the affective continuum.

   1. Jane can receive others as co-workers.
   2. Fred can comply with a directive.
   3. Sylvia can consume more liquids in a five minute period than Ralph can consume.
   4. Mrs. Thompson values honesty above all other virtues.

7. Select the item that would best fit under Category 3 of the affective continuum.

   1. "I like chocolate candy."
   2. "I disagree strongly with what you say, but I shall fight to the death for your right to say it."
   3. "What do you think of our foreign policy?"
   4. "Look, Billy is crying."

8. Select the item that would best fit under Category 4 of the affective continuum.

   1. I before E except after C.
   2. Knowing how to use a globe is important to a geographer.
   3. "If you don't do what I ask, I will be very angry."
   4. "Why would anyone value violence?"

9. Select the item that would best fit under Category 5 of the affective continuum.

   1. "I like cats."
   2. Plants would certainly die without proper moisture.
   3. "Based on the evidence being presented, I am willing to revise my judgment."
   4. To succeed in this world, it is important to identify with the majority opinion.

Chapter Three

A SYSTEMATIC APPROACH TO CLASSROOM ANALYSIS

TEACHING

The discussion of how best to teach has been going on since Cyrus Pierce, Henry Barnard, and others decided that formalized teacher preparation was necessary in a growing, changing society. Compulsory attendance laws brought a host of new problems. It meant keeping attendance records, spending more hours in school, giving extra help to slow learners, and teaching subjects new to the curriculum. The early 1800's represented a change in the responsibilities and scope of the school. The Three R's concept became outmoded due to the increased complexities of the society. Subjects such as nature study, music, manual training, science, and geography became staples of the curriculum. It became apparent that for teachers to adequately work with children in this changing society they would need a different and more extensive preparation.

The Industrial Revolution of the late 19th and 20th centuries created problems for the schools that still exist. The "knowledge explosion" has prompted the schools to explore new types and varieties of materials. An emphasis upon media and delivery systems, i.e. computers, as learning tools is most apparent. Subjects have entered the curriculum at a rapid rate. As society advances, the need to know more and more becomes a crucial problem. In essence, teachers must know more, and children must know more than ever before in our history. What began as a subject-centered curriculum remained. The movement toward child-centered curriculum continues to be a movement that seems destined to remain in second place. Institutions preparing future teachers have seen fit to offer more courses so that these students will have some acquaintance with the variety of subject areas they will be expected to teach.

Teaching is by its nature the process of changing behavior. Teachers are dedicated to providing opportunities for their students to grow intellectually, emotionally, and therefore, behaviorally. Arthur Combs, in his important book, *The Professional Education of Teachers* suggests that the effective helper or teacher is one who is constantly growing, re-evaluating his behavior, and creating an atmosphere whereby his students can follow suit. It follows therefore, that opportunities—many and varied—should be provided to teachers—preservice and inservice—in order that they may have the chance to experiment, to grow, to learn, to change, and to evaluate their own personal behavior.

Substantiating the existence of teaching is not difficult as it needs no defense. And yet, controversy is apparent. Of course, controversy, by its nature, need not be bad or harmful. What this discussion seems to be about is not why *have* teachers, but rather, why aren't teachers and the schools in general turning out a better product.

This writer assumes that a primary objective of all teachers will be to transmit information to the learner. However, I do not accept this objective as an entity unto itself. It would seem apparent, at least here, that there is more to teaching than being a dispenser of information. Mager has suggested that teachers have set themselves up as "infinite bags of knowledge." He suggests that we have seen ourselves as being able to dispense all the wisdom of the ages and, therefore, any learner wishing to know anything need only ask. I suspect that some of us are "infinite bags." However, what knowledge we transmit may be open to question.

There are some who would suggest that what we really need to do as effective teachers is to learn to love and be sensitive to the needs of our learners. Very few of us would argue this point. However, as Bruno Bettelheim points out, "Love is Not Enough." The "professional" teacher is—in addition to being a subject-matter specialist and a lover of people—a student of teaching. In order to accomplish this formidable task it will be necessary to examine teaching in other ways.

OBJECTIVE #1 – STUDYING CHILDREN

At present our methods of observing children seem haphazard at best. It is true that many teacher-education institutions offer courses in human growth and development—and tied in with these courses is observation. It is recognized further that those institutions who possess a four-year developmental program have built into the learners' experience opportunities to observe. Those universities whose education program is upper-divisional have included observation—but to a lesser degree. It should be pointed out, however, that a good deal of this observation has taken place in laboratory schools or those public schools designated by the college as appropriate. The term "appropriate" usually means those schools that will permit students from the college to come in. In many instances these situations are artificial and far removed from what goes on in most school rooms today. In essence, our student-learners are being sent out to unreal situations and told to "observe." Upon returning to the classroom, the student is expected to be able to discuss what he saw. The experience of this writer has indicated that many students cannot fulfill this requirement as they have not been taught to be trained observers. It's tough to have to look at something if you don't know what you're looking for, or at. It follows, therefore, that teachers are inexperienced in the techniques of observation since they have received little or no background preparing them to carry on this activity.

Gordon[1] suggests that the task of the teacher today is to develop readiness and enhance intelligence. He goes on to say that, "if what a teacher does in school is derived from his concepts of children and learning, then he must develop these new concepts." What Gordon seems to be suggesting is that for a teacher to develop concepts of children and learning, guided observation—conducted by skilled observers armed with, and knowledgeable of, observational techniques—is mandatory.

Developing new concepts using observational situations need direction. This direction should come from those personnel who are familiar with the various observational systems now being made available. Following through with this idea should provide teacher-educators with logical steps to follow:

1. Identify those members of the faculty interested in, and knowledgeable of, these new developments.

2. Work with personnel in a training program in an attempt to familiarize them with these strategies, and as a result provide for them ways of observing child behavior as well as their own behavior.

3. Graduate programs could be developed in an effort to train those individuals in systems analysis. Hopefully these graduates would then be brought into our schools as either supervising teachers or college supervisors of student teaching.

4. Another possible use of observation analysis would be for the improvement of college instruction. Since students do emulate teachers they have had, it seems imperative that professors of education and professors in general be constantly evaluating their own performance.

---

[1] Ira Gordon, *Studying the Child in School.* (New York: Wiley and Sons, Inc., 1966), p. 3.

OBJECTIVE #2 – STUDYING INSTRUCTION

Having available methods of analyzing teacher behavior is rather new and many teachers are not familiar with their use. Therefore, teachers have resorted to pencil and paper tests in an effort to evaluate their own performance. The assumption is made that if children do well on an exam, the content was learned and assimilated. Little thought is given to what the teacher did to stimulate and/or retard learning. What we have left to work with is a teacher lesson plan which is nothing more than an outline of procedure and gives few clues as to whether the teaching will be successful. As a result, many lessons have become technical and rather methodical.

We have available today for our use the results of research which has dealt with teacher behavior in its various aspects. What is being suggested here is that teachers consider the following procedures in an effort to be provided with more information about themselves. We do not hold that any of the suggestions made here will by themselves give total information but will rather supply to the teachers various avenues of self-evaluation.

Ned Flanders examined teacher behavior by means of his Interaction Analysis.[2] In this system the observer instantaneously categorizes teacher and pupil behavior into one of ten designated classes. This system does take training and may not be appropriate without special electronic equipment.

Arno Bellack analyzed teacher behavior as it affects teacher talk. By utilizing his scale an observer can classify what kinds of talk goes on in the classroom and direct this dialogue into four categories:

1. **Structuring** – describes how the teacher focused attention on the subject matter.

2. **Soliciting** – describes how the teacher elicits verbal response.

3. **Responding** – describes how the teacher reacts to the soliciting move.

4. **Reaction** – describes how the teacher accepts, rejects, modifies, or expands on what has been said earlier.[3]

---

[2]Ned Flanders. *Teacher Influence, Pupil Attitudes and Achievement.* (Washington, D.C.: Cooperative Research Monograph No. 12).

[3]A. A. Bellack and J. T. Davitz, *The Language of the Classroom: Meanings Communicated in High School Teaching.* (New York: Teachers College, Columbia University, U.S. Office of Education Projects N. 1497, 1963).

Ryan's study of teacher characteristics includes a rating scale that differentiates teachers on three patterns:

> **Pattern Xo** – warm, understanding, friendly versus aloof, egocentric, restricted teacher behavior.
>
> **Pattern Yo** – responsible, businesslike, systematic versus evading, unplanned, slipshod teacher behavior.
>
> **Pattern Zo** – stimulating, imaginative, surgent versus dull, routine teacher behavior.[4]

The judgment of the observer is a critical factor here, but since judgment is what supervisory staff rely on, this scale does provide a more systematized procedure.

The work of Medley and Mitzel (Oscar), Brown (TPOR, Taxonomy of Cognitive Behavior), Kaplan (Taxonomy of Affective Behavior), and others provide other vehicles by which behavior can be studied and analyzed. (The TAB will be discussed in Chapter Four.)

Of course each and all of these scales are subject to questions and therefore substantiate the point that these measures must be used as they are needed. However, they do supply evidence that can be used with other data to substantiate or refute an opinion.

Probably the most widely used method of observing teachers has been the use of simulation. Many teaching programs are now recording on video tape bits of teaching that can be replayed for the benefit of the teacher. In this way the teacher can more readily observe what went on during the lesson and thereby evaluate her own performance.

Evaluating the teacher has been a perennial problem for supervisors. However, being able to observe one's own behavior and therefore being able to self-analyze, seems the most appropriate of methods. This method tends to reduce the amount of talk that a supervisor must do about a situation that is already stale and difficult to remember.

Hopefully, we are approaching the time when teaching can be respected as a science as well as an art. Therefore, teachers are responsible for looking at their position in a scientific manner and analyzing those components that determine successful instruction. Teaching is not done haphazardly and should not and must not be observed in this manner.

---

[4]D. Ryans, *Characteristics of Teachers*. (Washington, D.C.: American Council on Education, 1960).

OBJECTIVE #3 – STUDYING ONE'S SELF

As we observe children and instruction we must invariably project ourselves into the situation. The performance of children is directly related to the effectiveness of the teacher. How good the teacher is becomes the key factor in a successful learning experience. Of course, in great part, a successful teacher is one who has to a great degree studied what has been referred to as objectives one and two. But in the long run a child learns best by identifying himself to someone who he admires, respects, and appreciates; the teacher knowing this, as teachers should, suggests that as individuals we are responsible to our learners.

Many students at the college level are quick to admit that their choice of course was predicated on who was teaching it. Of course, it is easy to say that students will look for the easy marker or soft touch, but this is not true. What our students are saying is that they are most willing to work hard when the learning has meaning. Students are wise to select professors whom they feel will provide for them the best learning opportunities.

"We do not listen to nonentities and we do not hear lightweights. I have often observed in my classes that communication between me and my students increases in direct proportion to the degree of earned authority I hold in their eyes. By earned authority I do not mean by titles or the books I have written. I earned these to be sure, but not with my students. By earned authority, I mean the authority my students invest in me as a consequence of their personal discovery of who I am, what I believe, and whether what I have to say is important. I do not have this earned authority when I meet these students for the first time. All I have then is my unearned authority: my degrees, my reputation, and the catalog designation that I am boss of this course. So long as these unearned authorities are in ascendance in our relationship, students hardly hear what I say. Accordingly, they dutifully write things down because if they did not, they would forget them. Later, when they know me better, and if I have earned my place as teacher in their eyes, they do not bother to write down much. We do not forget what important people have to say to us."[5]

Dr. Combs offers to teachers a direct challenge. Are we the people that our students will seek out? What is it about us that students feel they need? The need for all of us to look into ourselves for these answers is apparent.

Teachers must think about what they are doing *to* people. For too long, our concerns have been, "What can I do about children?" or "Why won't they learn?" These questions need concern but actually they are the wrong questions.

---

[5]Arthur W. Combs, *The Professional Education of Teachers.* (Boston: Allyn and Bacon, Inc., 1965), p. 69.

What needs to be asked is, "What am I? What do I have to offer children? Am I a person that children need? Would I want my own children to have me as their teacher?" When students are asked to define what qualities they see as necessary in a good teacher, these criteria very much take on what makes for a good human being. This is a far cry from those teachers who view themselves as dispensers of information or strict disciplinarians or any other label that we can hide behind. For this reason it is suggested that within teacher preparation, preservice and inservice, experiences be provided that will permit such introspection.

Effective counseling can be an enormous help in helping us understand ourselves. This should be handled by those trained individuals who see teaching as a personal thing and have themselves viewed their personalities through a looking glass.

Time must be provided to teachers to permit them to look at what is going on in their classroom and their responsibility to it. It would seem more appropriate to use faculty meetings for this purpose than to take the time now used for faculty meetings dicussing those things that usually can be decided by a competent secretary.

Combs suggests that the following areas are crucial in the perceptual organization of a good teacher:

1. Rich, extensive, and available perceptions about his subject field.

2. Accurate perceptions about what people are like.

3. Perceptions of self, leading to adequacy.

4. Accurate perceptions about the purpose and process of learning.

5. Personal perceptions about appropriate methods for carrying out his purposes.[6]

It is urged that this task of self-analysis begin at once. We've gone too long without it. Colleges of education have assumed that public school teachers possess these competencies and therefore have directed their attentions to the students working in the schools. This assumption is faulty and lacks evidence in its support. In fact, the data that is available suggests quite clearly that teachers feel inadequate and need support in their role as teachers. Kaplan's study (1966) indicates that teaching programs fall short as they relate to the inservice training of teachers and prospective teachers. In fact,

---

[6]*Ibid.*, p. 20.

interview data collected in this study point to the fact that these teachers ask for help but receive little or none.

SUMMARY

Those of us who have been trying to understand the teaching act have been drowned with the amount of information that is available. The problem seems to be to discover what the information means and where it fits. The benefit of the observational system is that it provides a schema for the theoretical construct and, in doing so, gives functional data that can be studied and then operationalized. It does this by permitting the learner to analyze and evaluate his own behavior—a behavior that has been defined and dissected into its basic components. The system permits the learner to examine his own theory and to make judgments. It is immediate and gives feed-back.

We need to know more about the teaching act. We need to know why some things work and others do not. If we are to be accountable for what we do, and we will be held accountable, then we must be prepared to describe the behavior of our students as well as our own behavior. Once we stop learning about what we do and stop trying to do more, I suspect that is the time to call it a day. The position of this chapter has been to encourage the investigator in pursuing his course and hopefully providing some direction to follow. We need to continue the search and I, for one, welcome those who desire to help us discover some answers.

REVIEW OF CHAPTER THREE

1. Define effective teaching. Attempt to put your thoughts into two paragraphs. (Use space provided for your comments.)

2. What is meant by the phrase, "love is not enough," as used in this chapter?

3. List six feed-back systems for teachers described in this chapter.

   a. _____

   b. _____

   c. _____

   d. _____

   e. _____

   f. _____

4. Define the phrase, "systematic analysis of teaching."

Chapter Four

THE TAXONOMY OF AFFECTIVE BEHAVIOR (T.A.B.)

A thorough investigation of the literature has produced evidence to support the notion that educational objectives can be classified into three major domains:

1. **Cognitive:** Objectives which emphasize remembering as well as solving intellectual tasks.

2. **Affective:** Objectives which emphasize a feeling, an emotion, a value, or a degree of acceptance or rejection.

3. **Psychomotor:** Objectives which emphasize some muscular or motor skill, some manipulation of materials and objects or some act which requires muscular coordination. (See *Taxonomy of Educational Objectives*. Bloom, Krathwohl, et al).

Observational systems pertaining to the cognitive and psychomotor aspects of teacher behavior have been developed. Many of these instruments are now in use and are providing important data. However, there are few, if any, systems dealing with the affective domain. It is from this need that the *Taxonomy of Affective Behavior* (T.A.B.) has been developed. This system was conceived and developed in an attempt to clarify and make operational the Krathwohl taxonomy. As a research tool, *Handbook II* is limited in its power to address those behaviors that can be produced under actual classroom situations. Putting it another way, it does not provide to the observer the breakdown of affective behaviors that may take place in the classroom and, in addition, does not provide the framework to note their occurrence.

The TAB consists of five categories, each representing a hierarchy of affective behaviors. These categories are consistent with the Krathwohl model. Each category has within it these affective behaviors that can be assigned to either teacher or student.

TOT	I		II		III		IV		V		RECEIVING (ATTENDING)
T P	T	P	T	P	T	P	T	P	T	P	**Awareness**
											1. Listens to others
											2. Receives others as co-workers
											3. Listens to advice
											4. Verbally pays attention to alternative points of view on a given issue
											5. Refers to subgroup(s) (social, intellectual, sex, race, etc.)
											6. Acknowledges some aesthetic factor in the classroom (clothing, furn., design, arrangement, art)
											7. Aware of feelings of others (introvert, extrovert, anxiety, hostility, sensitivity)
											8. Recognizes own bias as a bias
											9. Recognizes other bias as a bias

Figure 1. Mechanics for Scoring TAB[1]

MECHANICS FOR RECORDING DATA

The TAB provides a framework for observing and recording the affective behavior of the teacher and students in the classroom. The role of the observer is to watch and listen for signs of the behaviors described and to record whether or not they were observed. (Since it is the purpose of this instrument to provide feed-back to the teacher in order for him/her to make judgments, it is necessary to have a recorder, either colleague or supervisor, or some mechanical device, audio or video recorder, to provide feed-back.)

There are five separate seven-minute observation and marking periods in each 35 minute visit to the classroom. These are indicated by the column headings I, II, III, IV, and V (See Figure 1).

During period 1, the observer will spend the first five minutes observing the behavior of the teacher and students. In the next two minutes the observer

---

[1]The entire instrument is presented in Appendix A.

will go down the list of items and place a check (✓) in the T column (teacher behavior) and/or P column (pupil behavior) beside all items identified. As the observer becomes more familiar with the TAB it will be possible to observe and record simultaneously. For both teacher and pupil behavior, each item should be considered and marked with a ✓. A particular item is marked only once in a given column, no matter how many times that behavior occurs within the seven-minute observation period.(*)

Repeat this process for the second seven-minute period, marking in Column II. Repeat again for the third, fourth, and fifth seven-minute periods, marking in Columns III, IV, and V. The observer then adds the total number of ✓'s recorded in Column I through V for each teacher or pupil behavior and records this in the Column head TOT (Total). There may be from zero to five ✓'s for each item. By examining each column, the teacher is able to determine which behaviors were triggered by him/her or by the pupils. The teacher is then provided feed-back that can substantiate or refute the fulfillment of the goals established for the particular lesson.

The theory underlying the development of the TAB is built upon two hypotheses:

1. A teacher who becomes more sensitive to his or her own value system and can observe those values objectively will be sensitive to and help the student develop his or her own set of values.

2. The effective use of this instrument can produce a threat-free environment conducive to increased learning and creativity on the part of the individual student rather than forcing the teacher's own value structure upon the student.

Glossary of Behaviors Used in the TAB

1. Listens to Others

The individual indicates that alertness is present by some overt action.

Example:

A. The person looks at the speaker and verbally responds.
Pupil: "May I go to the boy's room?"
Teacher: "Yes."

---

*Note to reader: You may not wish to use all five of the recording columns at a given time. The 35-minute use provides a general overview of behavior for most lessons taught, however, it is appropriate to record for just one, two, or fewer than five segments.

Note: The teacher has listened by responding accordingly.

B. The person looks at the speaker and responds nonverbally.
Teacher: "Tim, please put that math problem on the blackboard."
Pupil: Tim gets out of his seat, goes to the blackboard and proceeds to write out the math problem.

Note: The pupil has listened by responding nonverbally.

2. Receives Others as Co-Workers

To acknowledge another person's presence.

Teacher: "Val, may Billy work along with you on your map?"
Pupil: "Aw, . . . uh . . . I suppose so."

Note: The pupil has received another learner to work along with her. She has not committed to anything beyond this acknowledgement. Also note that the pupil's response triggers behavior number 1, listens to others. It is very common that triggering one item will also trigger others.

3. Listens to Advice

Being aware that alternatives are available. The person needs to receive the information and show some overt action.

Teacher: "Don't just do something, think about what you are doing."
Pupil: "I'll try."

Note: The pupil has acknowledged the teacher's comment. However, it remains to be seen if he does anything about it.

4. Verbally Pays Attention to Alternative Points of View on a Given Issue

The listener shows awareness between alternative points of view by appropriate verbal response.

Teacher: "Who can tell us what constitutes a good breakfast?"
Pupil: "I have cold cereal and milk. I think that's a good breakfast."
Pupil: "I think that you need something warm to start the day."
Pupil: "Whether I have a cold or warm breakfast depends on the weather. Warm weather, cold breakfast. Cold weather, hot breakfast."

Note: The last pupil hit the mark.

5. Refers to Subgroups

Shows awareness of differences (social, intellectual, sex, race, age, etc.).

Teacher: "Would reading group I (the Pussywillows) please bring their chairs up front?"
Pupil: "Must I sit next to a girl?"

Note: Both teacher and pupil have demonstrated this behavior.

6. Acknowledges Some Aesthetic Factor in the Classroom

Alertness to available stimuli, i.e., clothing, furniture, art arrangement, etc.

Teacher: "Will all children with red sneakers please go to their seats."
Pupil: "That bulletin board looks attractive."

Note: Both teacher and pupil triggered the behavior.

7. Aware of Feelings of Others

Alertness to attitudes, i.e., introvert, extrovert, anxiety, hostility, sensitivity.

Pupil: "Miss Jones, Sally is crying."
Teacher: "What's wrong, Sally?"

Note: The teacher has shown some awareness that something is wrong. However, she has not yet gone beyond the awareness level.

8. Recognizes Own Bias as a Bias

Ability to state likes and dislikes without giving reasons or explanations.

Teacher: "I think Sally is sick."
Pupil: "She doesn't look sick to me."

Note: Both teacher and pupil have exhibited this behavior.

9. Recognizes Other Bias as a Bias

Can discriminate another person's likes and dislikes without necessarily knowing their reasons.

Pupil 1: "I can't stand poetry."
Teacher: "I enjoy poetry very much."
Pupil 2: "I agree with Jimmy. Poetry is for the birds."

Note: Pupil number 2 is aware that there are two opinions. He has selected one of these opinions as his own.

10. Seeks Agreement From Another

This implies a one-way answer.

Teacher: "Joan, would you please sit down."
Pupil: "May we go outside to play now?"

Note: Teacher and pupil have demonstrated this behavior.

11. Seeks Responsibility

Overtly demonstrate that there is a willingness to take charge of something.

Teacher: "May I help you with that algebra problem?"
Pupil: "May I erase the blackboard?"

Note: Teacher and pupil have demonstrated this behavior.

12. Seeks Information from Another

Shows by overt action that he/she needs facts which another person may have.

Teacher: "How many children brought their milk money today?"
Pupil: "What time is the band concert?"

Note: Teacher and pupil have demonstrated this behavior.

13. Pursues Another Way of Doing Something

Changing an existing structure.

Example: The teacher changes the lecture seating formation to a circular formation.

Teacher: "Who can think of another way of doing that problem?"
Pupil: "I believe that equation can be solved by multiplying rather than adding."

Note: Teacher and pupil have demonstrated this behavior.

14. Seeks Materials

Explores different sources of information.

Teacher: "Let's look it up in the dictionary."
Pupil: Goes to the class library and uses an encyclopedia (nonverbal).

Note: Teacher and pupil have demonstrated this behavior. Also note that nonverbal behavior is overt.

15. Asks Another to Examine Aesthetic Factor in Classroom

Action showing that the individual is sensitive to another person's view on sensual stimuli.

Teacher: "Martha, since you like purple, why don't you try to incorporate that color into your painting?"
Pupil: "How do you like the teacher's tie?"

Note: Teacher and pupil have demonstrated this behavior.

16. Inquires How Another Feels About Event or Subject

Asks how another person responds to some fact but the person's response need not cause a change in his/her feelings.

Teacher: "Did you like what you had for lunch?"
Pupil: "Did you enjoy the football game?"

Note: Teacher and pupil have demonstrated this behavior.

17. Complies with Existing Regulations (Rules)

Pays attention to directives in an overt manner which indicates that the directive is being followed.

Teacher: "Marvin, please get my attendance register. I have to have it with me when we leave for a fire drill."
Pupil: Student raises hand before speaking (nonverbal).

Note: Teacher and pupil have demonstrated this behavior.

18. Complies to a Suggestion or Directive

The person understands the situation and the consequences of compliance to the situation.

Teacher: "Deena, speak up."
Pupil: Learner complies in a louder voice.

Note: The pupil has demonstrated this objective.

Pupil: Learner asks teacher for assistance.
Teacher: Teacher verbally or nonverbally agrees to assist the learner.

Note: The teacher has demonstrated this objective.

19. Offers Materials on Request

The materials offered upon request are appropriate to the situation.

Pupil: "I'm confused about this theory."
Teacher: "Why don't you take a look at this book and see if it can help?"

Note: The teacher has demonstrated this objective. The teacher in this example has inferred from the student's comment that he/she is requesting some materials or assistance.

Teacher: "Can any of you add anything further to our discussion?"
Pupil: "I have an article that presents a different view of the situation."

Note: The pupil has demonstrated the behavior.

20. Gives Opinion when Requested

Complies to a request with a definite point of view.

Teacher: "Toni, do you think that a woman can get elected President of the United States?"
Pupil: Not only do I think a woman can get elected, but I also believe she would do much better than a man.

Note: The pupil has demonstrated this behavior with a definite point of view.

21. Responds to a Question

The response is a spontaneous opinion.

Pupil 1: "Do you think that smoking is harmful?"
Pupil 2: "No, I don't."
Teacher: "Well, I do."

Note: Pupil 2 and the teacher have demonstrated this behavior. Remember triggering this behavior will also trigger other behaviors such as 1.

22. Takes Responsibility When Offered

Complies to a request rather than offering.

Teacher: "Val, will you clean the blackboard?"
Pupil: Child responds by getting up and going to the blackboard.

Note: This behavior must be demonstrated by some overt action.

23. Remains Passive When a Response is Indicated

Actively ignores the appropriate response.

Teacher: "Joshua, please shut the door."
Pupil: (remains seated).
Pupil: "May I sharpen my pencil?"
Teacher: (does not respond).

Note: Personally, this type of behavior can get on your nerves.

24. Actively Rejects Directions or Suggestions

The person shows by some overt behavior that she holds a different opinion by either not complying or by complying with protest.

Teacher: "Evelyn, sit down!"
Pupil: Continues standing.
Teacher: "Evelyn, I'm not going to tell you again. Sit down!"
Pupil: Remains standing.

Note: Please do not hit Evelyn, even though the temptation is great.

25. Seeks the Value of Another

An attempt to discover how someone else feels about a certain thing and the degree of commitment assigned to the idea.

Teacher: "Why do you feel that marijuana should be legalized?"
Pupil: "How can you lecture on the evils of smoking when you smoke cigarettes?"

Note: The emphasis here is on discovery of feelings. This goes beyond asking a question for informational purposes.

26. Defends Value of Another

To support the value of another by verbally admitting a commitment to the same feeling, although the commitment to the feeling may not be held on an equal basis by both people.

Teacher: "I agree with the American Cancer Society's position on cancer and smoking. I recognize my weakness for smoking, however, that does not prohibit me from supporting their view."

Note: Do as I say rather than as I do.

27. Clearly Expresses a Value

Verbally states a feeling or attitude and gives reasons for having the feeling. The person expresses the worth for the value.

Teacher: "Cheating is morally wrong. Anyone who cheats is too stupid and immature to get by on his own."

Note: The difference between this behavior and just stating an opinion is at the level of commitment. A value is a high level of commitment expressed in strong feelings.

28. Defends Own Value

The person is motivated to state his/her feelings and to give reasons because the worth of these feelings may be challenged.

Pupil: "I agree. Cheating is wrong. However, with competition being what it is, sometimes the average student is forced into doing things he wouldn't normally do."

Teacher: "There is no excuse acceptable. If a student cheated his way through high school, how is he ever going to make it through college? How will he make it through life?"

Note: The teacher really means it.

29. Openly Defends the Right of Another to Possess a Value

The person supports the right of another to express his/her own value but may not have that value in his/her own system of values. The person demonstrates that he/she values the opportunity of others to express and hold their values.

Pupil: "I don't value that, but if you want to, go right ahead."
Pupil: "Jerry's a sissy because he wants to play in the doll corner. Boys don't play with dolls."
Teacher: "In this room he has the right to choose whatever activity he likes. And anyhow, who says that boys can't like dolls?"

Note: This teacher is not sexist.

30. Tries to Convince Another to Accept a Value

The person makes an effort to change another person's value.

Pupil: "If you don't stop playing with those stupid dolls, I'm not going to play with you any more. Playing with dolls is dumb."

Note: The teacher may not be a sexist but there is much work to be done.

31. Agrees with the Value of Another

The person has the same degree of commitment to the value that another person possesses.

Pupil: "My father is a pacifist. I believe, along with him, that stronger gun control legislation and effective enforcement is the only viable means to the reduction of killing and violence in this country."

Note: Just a reminder. There must be a high level of feeling expressed for this behavior and others in the valuing category to be triggered.

32. Disagrees with the Value of Another

Verbally rejects the value with supporting reasons for the rejection. The person is not rejecting the right of the other individual to possess the value.

Teacher: "I disagree with your position. I feel that this nation made a definite commitment to Southeast Asia and it would have been disastrous to our prestige not to have been involved to the degree we were involved."

Note: Sometimes teachers hold interesting values. However, I respect his right to believe what he does.

33. Makes Deductions from Abstractions

The person infers a value by recognizing a behavior which indicates a specific value. For example, a student knows and can say the words clean and dirty. He can point to a dirty shirt and label it as such. He is capable of verbally defining the behavior which typifies the value.

> Pupil: "My mother lets me play outside in the mud sometimes. If dirt were bad for me, my mother wouldn't let me play in it."

Note: Being able to perform at this level has high dividends. Students will do equally well in cognitive behaviors well up on that dimension.

34. Makes Judgments (Implies Evaluation)

The student can isolate certain characteristics of a concept and can examine the worth of these characteristics in relationship to his/her own values. This often lacks objectivity and may therefore suggest bias. The student for example, talks about the cleanliness of an object by saying, "that object is dirty." Or, "that object is clean." Or, "that object is cleaner than this object."

> Pupil: "My shirt's cleaner than your shirt. My shirt's better than your shirt."
> Teacher: "Nice children don't yell in the classroom."

Note: In each example, a value is clearly being expressed. The first example values cleanliness. The second values quiet or at least, no yelling. Both pupil and teacher have made judgments based on these values.

35. Compares Own Value to that of Another

The individual examines his/her own and others' values in order to discover the similarities and differences contained within these values.

> Teacher: "Our classroom is a mess. Ms. Dumas's boys and girls would never let their room get this way."

Note: The teacher in this example has really pointed out a similarity and a difference between the two classrooms. Both teachers seem to value cleanliness. This they have in common. However, their approach to achieving this goal varies considerably.

36. Attempts to Identify the Characteristics of a Value or Value System

The individual examines his/her and others' values in order to place them in a hierarchy or system of values.

> Pupil: "If he had the money, my father would redecorate the house. I would rather bank the money for my security in old age. This is more important than furniture."

Note: Both father and child value money. The pupil has examined both his own value and that of his father and prioritized them for his own purposes, consistent with his own beliefs.

37. Compares and Weighs Alternatives

To be cognitively aware of the consequence of adopting certain values and weighing these against each other.

> Pupil: "If I let my hair grow, my parents will be upset. If I keep it short, I won't be in the in-crowd. I want to be in the in-group, so I'll let my hair grow."

Note: The student has decided how much effort must be put into letting his hair grow long, and whether or not he values his parents more than he wants the approval of other students in his school. He has examined the issues and made his choice.

38. Shows Relationship of One Value to Another

The student can define the cause and effect or any overlap of two separate values. For example, the student may not have enough money to buy soap. He therefore may come to school dirty and be criticized by his teacher. He may conclude that being dirty and disapproval are caused by a lack of money. Value placed on material things and cleanliness overlap.

> Teacher: "If you don't brush your teeth, you'll get cavities. I know that your parents don't have the money to spare right now for extra trips to the dentist. If you brush your teeth, you not only prevent cavities but you'll be saving your parents money."

Note: In the first example, it is possible that the student may confuse a lack of funds with disapproval. Learners must be assisted if they are to be able to develop the skills involved in this behavior. They can easily become confused.

39. Ties a Specific Value Into a System of Values

Acceptance into a group is more important than approval by the individual or others outside of the desired population. For example: The student may wish to violate the norm and wear dirty clothes in order to be accepted by a person or persons he admires. In addition, he/she may also compromise in order to fit that value in a higher set of values.

> Pupil: "If I let my hair grow long my parents will be upset. If I keep it short, I won't be in the in-crowd. I really don't want my hair long, so I'll buy a wig."

Note: This student has learned the art of compromise. This can prove to be a valuable tool in the interactions we all have with other people.

40. Synthesizes Two or More Value Into One Value

This implies a great deal of creativity. Example: Cleanliness and attractiveness create a sense of well being which promotes over all good health. The new value created may be that good health is desirable.

Note: Creating a situation whereby a third student, after observing two other students state their values, can demonstrate this skill is but one way to work this behavior into an everyday teaching/learning situation.

41. Revises Judgments Based on Evidence

Reconsiders own thinking and places a new degree of commitment on an old value in light of documented facts.

Pupil: "The recent research supports what I've been saying all along. Smoking is dangerous to your health. It is bad."

Note: Editorial comment. It would be lovely if more teachers and students demonstrated this behavior. Just imagine a world where people were willing and able to change their minds when presented with evidence.

42. Bases Judgments on Consideration of More Than One Proposal

Elements of using another person's plan as a base of support for a decision.

Example: Other pupils offer suggestions and the first student comes to a decision based on bits and pieces of other people's proposals.

Note: The individual checks all bases before making a decision.

43. Makes Judgments in Light of Situational Context

Comes to a decision based upon a one time happening. This could include revising an attitude in light of different facts; stronger commitment than the last two behaviors discussed. This becomes a part of the individual's intrinsic system.

44. Develops a Consistent Mode of Behavior

Another person can describe and predict the person's behavior in a given situation.

45. Continually Re-Evaluates Own Mode of Behavior

The ability to look at one's behavior objectively. This implies a criteria used in evaluating values and their components.

Note: The last three behaviors are not really in the same class or category as the others; they are more products of the others.

SUMMARY

The TAB is designed to produce most, if not all, of those measures described in the Krathwohl taxonomy. For the most part, category designations and definitions have been retained, but in certain instances, individual categories have been modified to reduce overlap between categories. Probably the greatest advantage to the TAB is that it provides direction to the learning process. It does this by providing terminology that is hopefully clear and meaningful. It is anticipated that the objectives classified in this observational instrument will provide to the learner those kinds of behaviors expected of students and teachers and, in addition, provide for them the direction and framework to assist in the acquisition of these skills. It is perhaps naive to hope that the TAB can reach this ideal because of the difficulties involved in using language to communicate, but the attempt is made to provide direction to this objective in so far as affective behavior in the classroom is concerned.

A second value derived from the TAB is to provide a convenient vehicle for students and teachers for describing their behavior and pointing out to them those areas that need development. If evaluation is to be meaningful, then it should take the form of self-analysis. This instrument provides the framework for learners to look at their own behavior and react accordingly.

Thirdly, by working with this instrument, it may be possible to discover some of the principles of ordering and/or classifying behaviors. This ordering can provide useful information leading toward a theory of learning and instruction applicable for classroom use.

Additionally, this instrument has the potential to help teachers develop curriculum. For example, rather than teaching a particular reading skill for the sake of that skill alone, the skill can be used to trigger or stimulate a higher level affective behavior as identified by this taxonomy. In this way, there is a correlation that can be shown between the achievement of the basic skill and the internalization of the behavior in the affective domain.

There is adequate reason to assume that teachers need to be trained to identify some of the more subtle and uncommon types of student and teacher behavior. Until they become aware and sensitive to a variety of behaviors, they may neither have the skill to identify nor the capability to produce these important forms of teacher-student behavior.

In 1983 Phyllis Beaver* completed a study in which she used "The Taxonomy of Affective Behavior in the Classroom" as the basis for a Internalization Model. She selected six behaviors from the taxonomy going in

---

*For further information the reader is advised to contact Phyllis Beaver, Covington Consulting, 33000 Covington Club Drive, Suite 37, Farmington Hills, Michigan 48018.

ascending order of commitment. She used this model to measure the level of commitment that workers have to performing affective behavioral skills on the job.

Steps of Internalization		
6	Make judgments in light of situational context	
5	Synthesizes two or more values into one value	
4	Makes judgments	
3	Agrees with the value of another	
2	Defends own value	
1	Clearly expresses a value	
Base Line	10 20 30 40 50 60 70 80 90 100	

Percentage of Internalization

The purpose of her study was to test the validity of the model. She used registration workers from ten community colleges in Michigan. Five of the colleges (experimental group) had used a training package to enhance the interpersonal relationship skills of their workers when working with students at registration. The other five colleges (control group) did not have the training.

Both the experimental and control groups completed questionnaires that attempted to elicit values rather than opinions. A group of raters (knowledgeable in the area of affect and trained on how to use the model) read each respondent's answers and rated them based on their level of commitment vis a vis the steps of the model. Results showed that there was a significant difference in the affective behavioral skills of the workers in these groups. The workers in the experimental group exhibited a higher internalization level than the workers in the control group.

Beaver's model is also very helpful when designing questionnaires for market research. It enables the researcher to elicit values rather than simply opinions. Thus, by using the model, it is possible to determine what level of commitment the respondents have to a particular value.

There are many other applications for Beaver's technique. Instructors can use their own imagination and probably think of many more. For those interested in identifying values in addition to opinions, the T.A.B. is a useable instrument. It is simply a tool, and when used correctly, it can be very effective.

REVIEW OF CHAPTER FOUR

The following episodes are provided as an opportunity to check your understanding of the Taxonomy of Affective Behavior. As you read each passage, note the particular behavior or behaviors triggered in that piece of dialogue. Parentheses are provided for this purpose.

Example #1

    P: "Miss Smith, I think Susan is crying!"
    T: "What's wrong Susan?" (7)

The teacher's response clearly indicates the triggering of item #7 on the TAB; aware of feelings of others.

Example #2

    T: "Cheating is wrong! Anybody that cheats is too stupid to get by on his own." (27)
    P: "I agree. Cheating is ridiculous." (26)

The teacher's response suggests she clearly values honesty (Item #27). The pupil's agreement is a clear example of Item #26; supports the value of another.

The reader is encouraged to use the TAB as a guide for this exercise. (See Appendix A.) An answer key is provided in the back of the book to check your responses against those of the "experts."

THE POETRY LESSON

1. T: "Thank you, Bettina. That was very nice. (   ) Steve, would you like to read our next poem?"

2. P: "No! (   ) I hate poems. (   ) They're sissy stuff. (   ) Only girls like that poetry junk." (   )

3. T: "Oh! I'm sure you'd really like to. This is such a nice poem about the flowers we see in Springtime. I know that you'll enjoy it." (   )

4. P: "I said I hated poems. (   ) They're sissy stuff. (   ) Only girls like that poetry junk." (   )

5. P: "Oh, Miss Smith. I don't know how he can feel that way. (   ) I feel that poetry is just beautiful—beautiful words, beautiful people, beautiful meanings." (   )

6. T: "Well . . . !"

7. P: "I'm with Steve. (   ) I haven't seen one poem in this old book of ours that looks any good at all." (   )

8. T: "I certainly am surprised to hear that so many of you boys feel this way. Let's have a show of hands to see just how many people don't like poetry. (Pause) I see. It seems like most of the class doesn't. Can anyone tell me why?" (   )

9. P: "Well, none of the poems we've read about talk about anything that's real. (   ), (   ) Remember that one about the silver tree in the silver moonlight? Well, I've never seen anything like that before."

10. T: "Well, let me ask you this. Suppose one night that you went out into your backyard and the moon was shining down. How would you describe what you saw?" (   )

11. P: "All I'd see would be a tree in the moonlight. (   ) Why can't they just keep things plain and simple. It sure would be easier to understand." (   )

12. P: "You know that Miss Smith told us last week that different people who write express themselves differently. It's the same in regular books. Everyone has a right to be different, or to do things in a different way." (   ), (   )

13. P: "I agree with Pam. (   ) I love to read books of poems, but I'd never ever read about frogs, for example."

14. P: "Boy, show me a poem about frogs and I'll read that. I like frogs! They jump really high and it's fun to watch their webbed feet work in the water. The other day, Bill and I had a frog race—mine won." (   )

15. P: "Oooo! How can you stand to touch an icky old frog? They give you warts. I wouldn't touch one for anything." ( )

16. P: "Me, neither. ( ) Girls ( ) hate frogs like poison." ( )

17. T: "Well, I don't know about that, Kimila. I think frogs are pretty interesting myself. Like Jack said, they do jump rather high. When I was a little girl, we used to have bullfrog croaking contests every Sunday afternoon. My granfather had the biggest frog around, so his always won." ( )

18. P: "Wow! That sounds like fun. Could we get some bullfrogs here?" ( )

19. T: "Well, why don't you call up the pet store and find out? ( ) Then you could report back to the class. Meanwhile, I think we've gotten just a little bit off the subject. Have any of you boys ( ) ever read any poems that are written especially for boys?" ( )

20. P: "How could any kind of poetry be for boys?" ( ), ( )

21. P: "Steve, think of some of the things you like to talk about." ( )

22. P: "Well, cowboys, horses, dogs, pirates . . . I can't think of anymore right now." ( )

23. P: "That's enough. Now, just take any of our poetry books and look through them. I bet you'll find lots of poems about those things you like." ( )

24. P: "Aw, I don't believe you." ( )

25. P: "Hey! Here's one about a cowboy named Bob. I think I'll read that tonight. They've even got a picture of a horse on the next page." ( )

26. P: "Hey! Can you find a poem for me? Is there one about fish? ( ) Not that I want to read it or anything like that, but I did get some new fish for my tank and I should find out what other people say about fish. ( ) That's the only way to learn more." ( )

27. T: "Well, now that we've taken care of all that, who is ready to read our next poem? (Pause) Well, I still don't see Steve and Jack raising their hands, but the rest of us will have to realize that not everyone likes the same things we do." ( )

28. P: "Miss Smith, this cowboy poem isn't really too bad. I still don't like all the flowery stuff. But anytime you find a poem about cowboys, I'll read it for you." ( )

Chapter Five

CURRICULUM ACTIVITIES

It is the objective of this chapter to have the reader practice what has been discussed thus far in the book. Hopefully, by going through the activities and then discussing each one either with a colleague or in your college class you will begin to understand how objectives in the affective domain can be utilized. In addition opportunities will be available to initiate your own objectives for your own students.

This chapter is divided into two sections. *Section one* will provide you the opportunity of seeing how teaching activities highly cognitive in nature can be easily transformed to pick up affective behaviors from the learners. *Section two* will provide a few examples of lesson plans that have been formulated to specifically trigger certain behaviors from the *Taxonomy of Affective Behavior*.

For additional practice in checking your accuracy with the T.A.B. an episode similar to one presented at the conclusion of Chapter Four is provided in Appendix B (The Date). This dialogue will provide you with another opportunity to check your scoring with the author as well as giving you more practice in using the T.A.B. as a feed-back instrument.

SECTION ONE – LESSON PLANS

The following lesson plans are designed to produce behaviors that are knowledge based. These plans do a reasonable job for what they are designed to produce. However, by adding some affective variables these lessons will not only give cognitive outcomes but will, in addition, produce affective outcomes as well. The result is two-fold: a lesson that develops affective dimensions and a lesson that produces additional cognitive outcomes beyond those originally designed.

Lesson Plan 1

TOPIC

Stored Energy

MATERIALS

1. Teacher
   a. Textbook
   b. Chalkboard
2. Students
   a. Textbook
   b. Pen or pencil and paper

OBJECTIVES

1. To develop the understanding of the way in which energy, which has been stored in the form of coal, oil, and gas, is converted into electrical energy.
2. To find out how the energy which is stored in coal is transformed into electrical energy.
3. To have students understand that the sun is the source of all energy.

PROCEDURE

1. Review the water cycle and the relation of the sun and the water cycle to the hydroelectrical power plant.
2. Have the students open their textbooks to page 167 and read from pages 167 to 171.
3. Through questions, establish that coal, oil, and gas, have stored energy that can be put to use to produce electrical power. Also, how coal was formed and during what period of time will also be discussed.
4. Have students explain the process of how coal is used to produce electrical power in the illustrations on pages 168-169.
5. Have the students outline this process step-by-step as given in the textbook.

CONCLUSION

A discussion of the two types of turbines correlate with this section on stored energy. Questions will be asked about the function of the turbine and its relationship with the generator.

COMMENTS

This lesson is fairly typical of many science lessons taught in the schools. There is a reliance upon the text for basic information. Questions formulated from the reading are asked the learners in an effort to assess their knowledge of the content contained in the book.

In order to place this lesson more into the affective continuum some value oriented questions might be explored.

1. Of what value is coal, oil, or gas to the average individual?
2. Is there a relationship between a coal miner's work stoppage and the average person's willingness to conserve energy?
3. In your judgment, (the student) what are the strengths and limitations of this country relying on foreign oil or natural gas?

By permitting the learners the opportunity of engaging in a discussion around these questions, the teacher should be able to assess the following:

a. the student's knowledge of subject matter;
b. the ability of the students to put the information contained in the text into some sort of construct having practical and relevant applications;
c. the ability of the students to make inferences;
d. the student's ability to make deductions from abstractions.

All of these objectives are possible because the teacher asked value or feeling oriented questions. As is the case in these matters, students must possess basic content knowledge to deal with these questions. The result is more information than possible in the lesson as described initially. As mentioned earlier, affect produces higher level cognitive behavior.

NOTES

Lesson Plan 2

TOPIC

1. To show children that birds must in some way prepare for winter in the fall.
2. To acquaint children with the birds that stay around our area in the winter.

MATERIALS

1. Film strip: "Birds Get Ready for Winter."
2. Pictures of birds: bobolink, chickadee, nuthatch, blue jay, mallard duck.
3. Ditto: "Birds Find New Homes."
4. Crayons

INTRODUCTION

We have been talking about how different people get ready for winter during the fall. Today we are going to talk about what birds do in the fall.

Show picture of the birds mentioned above.

Discuss migration of birds. Which birds remain here for the winter?

PROCEDURE

Show film strip. The following questions will be answered and discussed by entire group.

1. What is the availability of food for birds in the spring, summer, and fall?
2. What do they eat (seeds, worms, insects, berries)?
3. What can we do to help the birds that stay here for the winter (bird feeders, sprinkle food on the ground)?
4. Identify birds that go south (robin, blackbird, flicker, geese, bluebird, barn swallow, duck).
5. Identify birds that stay here (goldfinch, cardinal, blue jay, nuthatch, chickadee, crow, junco bird).
6. Other factors (goldfinch—grows white feathers; blue jay—hides acorns and beechnuts in the fall and by so doing he plants many trees. He/she also forgets where they were hidden.)

CONCLUSION

Ditto papers are distributed to children as they prepare for coloring. Color ditto. Add to "Fall Booklets."

COMMENTS

This lesson is informative and has the potential to be great fun. If the film strip is attractive the children will or should be able to identify the various birds described, answer the questions that follow and probably enjoy coloring the ditto. This lesson also has the potential of being very fact oriented and somewhat stifling from a creative point of view. If the teacher follows the lesson plan as described it is anticipated that the children will never go beyond the memorization level in dealing with the content. It is also anticipated that all birds will be colored alike and therefore look alike or very similar to the film strip.

It is suggested that by permitting or stimulating the children to pursue another way of doing something (Item #13 on the T.A.B.), a variety of drawings would appear that not only ask the children to color between the lines, but create a setting or environment for these drawings. This picture then ties the information presented by the film strip and the teacher into a form of evaluation which better determines if the children have internalized the lesson.

With some teacher direction the children could also be making some value judgments based on the information in the lesson (Item #34). A question such as, "from what you have learned today, what can you say about how people react to various seasons," permits the learner to draw inferences and therefore make evaluative, value oriented judgments.

Adding the two objectives (#13 and #34) to this lesson would have put this activity far more into the affective column and as is the case with most lessons, would have produced a higher level, more comprehensive cognitive payoff.

NOTES

Lesson Plan 3

TOPIC

Bean Mosaic

GOAL

To develop tracing skills; to use and develop fine motor skills and eye-hand coordination.

MATERIALS

Pencil, tracing paper, a simple line picture, glue, cardboard, and example of the finished product.

OBJECTIVE

Given tracing paper, a simple line picture and a pencil, the student will trace the picture with no more than 1/8" deviation. The student will then glue the traced picture to a given piece of cardboard without error.

PROCEDURE

1. Tell child what he will be making.
2. Show example of finished product.
3. Demonstrate steps: take picture, place tracing paper over it, tape to desk, trace, remove tape, show finished product.
4. Permit student to select picture.
5. Set up and/or assist child with tracing paper.
6. Have student repeat procedure until a satisfactory (deviation within 1/8") picture results.
7. Glue double-bonded traced picture onto cardboard.
8. Clean-up.
    a. put pencils away
    b. throw away used paper
    c. stack finished products
    d. put away glue—make sure tops are on tightly
    e. wash table if necessary.

EVALUATION

Students will be evaluated as to how well and how independently they performed the above tasks.

COMMENTS

This lesson was developed primarily for a group of mentally impaired children who seem to be having difficulty with activities that call upon their eye-hand coordination. Some classrooms of primary age youngsters have used this lesson for the same purpose but also to give practice to those needing help in following specific directions.

It is obvious that this lesson is totally teacher oriented. The children are all following the same directions at precisely the same time. Without observing the classroom it is safe to assume that not all of these youngsters need this practice to the same degree. The concept of individual differences between learners is still viable. By careful observation the teacher should be able to identify some in the class capable of performing these skills and equally capable of assisting their peers. In this manner these children in addition to sharpening these tools are learning responsibility (T.A.B. Item #22) as well as developing the value of assisting others in need of help (third category—Valuing). As in the case of all affectively oriented objectives, the product of these objectives is increased learnings for the pupils as well as a further developed commitment to others and themselves as individuals to be valued and appreciated.

NOTES

SECTION TWO – MORE LESSON PLANS
(But With a Difference)

The following lesson plans are provided as examples of how an affective orientation can stimulate affective and cognitive results. An opportunity is provided at the conclusion of each plan for the reader to make comments that may stimulate other teaching episodes in your classroom.

Lesson Plan 1

TOPIC

    Literature—*Huckleberry Finn*

GOAL

    The object of this lesson is to awaken the students to the process by which existing social attitudes are questioned and ultimately changed and in addition, to encourage them to open themselves to ideologies other than those they profess so that they can successfully defend their own beliefs. (Items #25, 27, and 28.)

PROCEDURE

1. After the work has been read, the class will be divided into groups of five or six students for the purpose of investigating the social environment that provides the background of the story. They will be encouraged to think about such questions as:

    a. What were the political philosophies of the day, especially in regards to blacks?

    b. What Christian values existed in the society?

    c. What social and cultural values were present in the society?

    d. What was the role of children in the society?

    e. Of women?

    Much of the information needed to answer these questions can be discovered in the text. The students will be expected to cite specific passages in support of their points of view. (One class period.)

2. After the period of investigation the class will come together in a circle to share their findings. During this sharing, the class will also discuss the literary devices used by Twain to create his story; thus, social, historical, as well as literary commentary will be discussed simultaneously.

3. The students will be asked to defend or refute any of the values, implicit or explicit, which are presented as a result of the work in part 1. This will, in a non-threatening way, ask them to expose their own biases and values. Those students who do not take a position initially, will be asked to align themselves with a student who has proposed a defense or refutation. This will create new groupings. (Parts 2 and 3, one class period.)

4. The opposite ideological position will be assigned each of the groups, i.e., if a group defended Huck's father's right to have Huck live with him, they will be told that they must defend Huck's position on freedom from a repressive and amoral parent. Each group will discuss the "other side" of the issue, trying to consider all the ramifications of the arguments. (One class period.)

5. The circle will be formed again and sharing of new insights will take place. (One-half to one class period.)

EVALUATION

The students will synthesize (Item #40) through brainstorming, a one-sentence or one-paragraph summary of what they have learned; every issue has at least two sides and no one can assume a position without listening to all reflections on each side of the issue.

The teacher will point out that literature is often a door by which an author makes a social statement and will then offer a list of books which are currently popular and supportive of that point. The students will be invited (but not assigned) to select, read and share their reflections on one of these books (or any other they feel makes a social statement) with the class.*

COMMENTS

Even though a few of the items on the T.A.B. have been highlighted, many others were stimulated through the discussion in the lesson. You might want to see how many you can discover.

---

*This plan calls for an entire week to be devoted to the study of *Huckleberry Finn* which is not an unusual period of time to discuss a full-length novel. This plan was developed by Carol Popp.

NOTES

Lesson Plan 2

TOPIC

Dimensions of Cooperation

OBJECTIVES

To stimulate the group to analyze some aspects of the problem of cooperation in solving a group problem.

To sensitize the members to some of their own behavior which contributes toward or hinders solving group problems.

MATERIALS

Individual tables that will seat five participants. One set of SQUARES for each five people participating. (See directions for making the sets of squares.) One set of INSTRUCTIONS for each five people participating and one for the leader.

ROOM ARRANGEMENT

If practical, tables should be arranged in advance with groups of five chairs around them and with a packet of the necessary materials on each table. The tables should be spaced far enough apart that the various groups cannot observe the activities of the other groups. The members then take chairs as they enter. If this is not practical, tables and chairs may be arranged after the leader's introduction.

DISCUSSION

This exercise involves so much interest and feeling that the group discussion usually carries itself, though the leader may need to guide the focus of comments or may wish to add points from his/her own observations.

The discussion should go beyond relating experiences and general observations. Some important questions are: How did members feel when someone holding a key piece didn't see the solution? How did members feel when someone had completed his square incorrectly and then sat back with a self-satisfied smile on his face? What feelings did they think he had? How did members feel about the person who couldn't see the solution as fast as the others? Did they want to get him out of the group or help him?

When the discussion is under way, the leader may wish to raise questions which stimulate the participants to relate their feelings and observations to their daily work experiences.

In summarizing, the leader briefly stresses the relationship of the experiences with squares and the discussion to back home work situations.

DIRECTIONS FOR MAKING A SET OF SQUARES

A set of five envelopes containing pieces of cardboard which have been cut in different patterns and which, when properly arranged, will form five squares of equal size. One set should be provided for each group of five persons. Since groups often run from 15 to 20 persons, it is suggested that the leader make four sets while he is about it.

To prepare a set, cut out five cardboard squares of equal size, approximately six by six inches. Place the squares in a row and mark them as below, penciling the letters a, b, c, etc., lightly so they can later be erased.

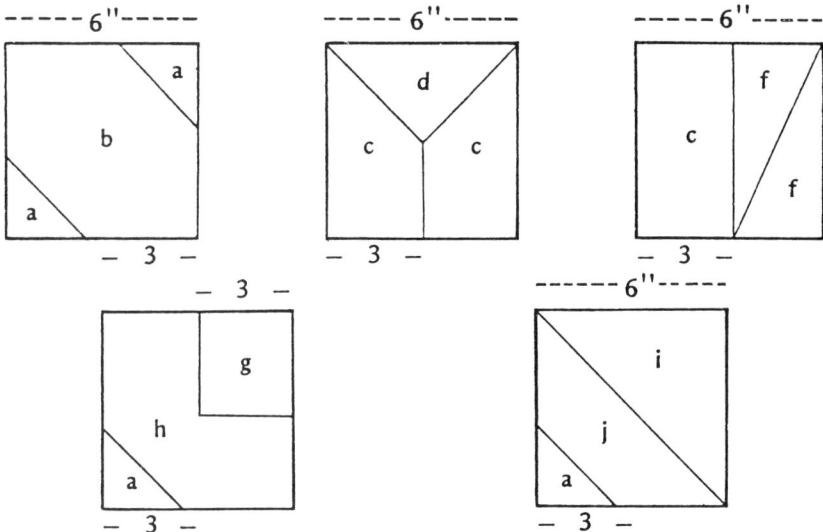

The lines should be drawn so that when cut, all pieces marked (a) will be of exactly the same size, all pieces marked (c), of the same size, etc. By using multiples of three inches several combinations will be possible that will enable participants to form one or two squares, but only one combination is possible that will form five squares six by six inches.

After drawing the lines on the six by six inch squares and labeling them with lower case letters, cut each square as marked into smaller pieces to make the parts of the puzzle. Mark each of five envelopes A, B, C, D, and E. Distribute the cardboard pieces in the five envelopes as follows:

Envelope A has pieces i, h, e
         B   a, a, g, c
         C   a, j
         D   d, f
         E   a, b, f, c

Erase the penciled letter from each piece and write, instead, the appropriate envelope letter, as Envelope A, etc. This will make it easy to return the pieces to the proper envelope for subsequent use when a group has completed the task.

INSTRUCTIONS TO THE GROUP

In this package are five envelopes, each of which contains pieces of cardboard for forming squares. When the signal to begin is given, the task of your group is to form five squares of equal size. The task will not be completed until each individual has before him a perfect square of the same size as that held by others.

Specific limitations are imposed upon your group during this exercise:

1. No member may speak.
2. No member may ask another member for a card or in any way signal that another person is to give him a card.
3. Members may, however, *give* cards to other members.

COMMENTS

This lesson has been frequently used in classrooms as well as in parlor games. The major strength of this activity is that it provides the opportunity for learners to understand the potential of cooperative behavior (Item #2).

NOTES

Lesson Plan 3

TOPIC

    Reading

    "Come Out Shadow, Wherever You Are"

    New Words: Shadow, okay, leader, disappeared

Story Summary:

    Davey is playing outside with his shadow when a cloud comes over and his shadow disappears. When Davey can't figure out where his shadow has gone he starts to follow an older boy's shadow. The older boy, Stanley, tells him to go home and tricks him into turning around so that Stanley can run away. Just as Davey figures out what has happened, the cloud moves away and Davey follows his shadow all the way home.

SPECIFIC OBJECTIVES

    In the Story:

    Understanding Literature

        Discovering clues to plot development

    Inferential Comprehension

        Predicting an outcome

        Using clues for interaction

    Literal Comprehension

        Recognizing details

    Word recognition of the new words through practice

    In the Study pages:

    Introduction to Contractions—Practice writing and using them

MATERIALS

1. Word cards for shadow, Davey, Stanley, disappeared, leader
2. Chalkboard
3. Copies of the two work sheets run off

IDENTIFYING PURPOSES FOR READING

    Pass out the books and let the children skim the title, cover, and glance through the book. If they would like to, allow them to talk to each other as they are doing this. When they seem to be finished, introduce the vocabulary words. The word cards can be used along the chalk ledge for an introduction. Discuss the definitions of the words and try making up a sentence using the words. Also introduce the two characters Davey and Stanley at this time. Begin a discussion of the cover of the book and see if the children can now figure out the title using the new word shadow. Lead a general discussion about shadows: What makes them? Why would they disappear? Can they occur at night? Can they occur on rainy days? Give the children time to discuss shadows until you are sure that they feel comfortable and are sure of the definition of a shadow.

Write the phrases: 'Follow the leader' and 'You're a copy cat!' on the board. Ask if anyone can tell you what these two say and then talk about the phrases to make sure everyone is clear on their meaning before the silent reading. These two phrases should start some discussion by the children because they are popular. (See discussion questions below.) You may start the discussion now or wait until the story is read as the children may then have more to relate to.

GUIDING THE ADJUSTMENT OF RATE TO PURPOSES AND MATERIAL

The children should now be asked to read the story to themselves. Give them as much time as they need and mention the fact that, if they have any problems with the words, they should ask you. This way help can be given on decoding problems individually.

OBSERVING THE READING AND DEVELOPING COMPREHENSION

Use your own judgment as to further work with the vocabulary. If the children are not having trouble with the new vocabulary, then there is no need for further work. Below is a list of questions that you may use as the children read the pages orally or may be used after the silent reading if the children do not read orally. However, the page-by-page questions are only concerned with literal comprehension. Following these questions is a section of discussion questions which will not only test comprehension but go beyond that to test how the happenings in the story might relate to the children and their lives. These questions should only be used to lead the discussion and not to rule it. The children should be allowed to come to their own conclusions, whether they are the ones you would like them to have or not.

The literal questions may seem tedious and so you may want to go right to the discussion section to alleviate boredom.

Page 1 – What is Davey doing? What else do you notice about the picture? What kind of day is it?

Page 2 – What type of things did Davey do with his shadow? What did Davey want the shadow to do?

Page 3 – What happened to the shadow? Why did the shadow disappear? What did Davey ask the shadow? What do you think Davey will do next?

Page 4 – What did Davey decide to do? Where did Davey follow Stanley's shadow? Why do you think that the shadow started moving faster?

Page 5 – What did Davey want the shadow to do? Did it? What did Davey do to try and stop the shadow? Does this stop the shadow? Can you stop a shadow by doing this?

Page 6 – What did Stanley tell Davey? What did Stanley finally say to Davey?

Page 7 – What did Stanley do? What did Davey say? How do you think Davey felt?

Page 8 – How do you think Davey feels now that his shadow has reappeared? How do you think Davey finally feels about Stanley?

DISCUSSION QUESTIONS

What do you think about the way Stanley treated Davey? Why do you think he might have been so mean? What makes you feel mean sometimes? Could Stanley have acted differently when Davey talked to him? Have you ever had bigger boys and girls be mean to you? How did it feel? Have you ever been mean to one of your younger brothers and sisters?

The discussion may go in this vein or may lead in other directions. However, the children should be able to discuss the story in relation to the life around them without adult interjections of "No, that isn't right," so be careful that you let them voice their opinions freely.

FUNDAMENTAL SKILL-TRAINING ACTIVITIES:
DISCUSSION, FURTHER READING,
ADDITIONAL STUDY, WRITING

You may find that the discussion above becomes very interesting for the children at which time role playing might also become a good vehicle for them to vent their feelings.

Below is a list of several books on shadows that the children should have available to them after reading the story. All of these books are readable for children reading at an approximate 2.1 level.

Mendoza, George, *Shadowplay.* Holt, Rinehart, and Winston, New York, 1973.

> Photographs of shadow images of swans, camels, Napoleon, witches and other figures together with photographs showing how the images are formed using hands and fingers.

Simon, Seymour. *Light and Dark.* McGraw-Hill, New York, 1970.
   An introduction to light and shadows.

Schwalberg, Carol. *Light and Shadow.* Mag. Press, 1972.
   An introduction to the principles of light.

Another idea for a follow-up is to take the children out on a sunny afternoon and let them find their own shadows. After they have played with their shadows or a friend's shadow, have them come back in and write their own stories about what happened to them and their shadows.

COMMENTS

This lesson should provide the learner another opportunity of seeing how affect can be instilled into a lesson that is very skill or knowledge oriented. Again, feelings and skill development are not incompatible.

NOTES

---

*This lesson plan was developed by Kristine Tracy. It was adapted from a story by Bernice Myers, *Come Out Shadow, Wherever You Are!* Scholastic Book Service, New York, 1970.

Chapter Six

BE CREATIVE

In this section you are asked to develop your own lesson plans. The pictures included in this chapter will stimulate ideas around which you may create indepth learning experiences for your students.

As you think about each teaching episode be careful not to attempt to trigger or highlight more than a few of the behaviors on the T.A.B. Others will occur as a natural consequence of the lesson. Focus in on what you believe will be of intellectual significance to the population you have in mind. *Remember:* The more sophisticated the behavior selected from the T.A.B. the greater the potential. (See Appendix A.)

Picture 1

Picture 1

Note to Teacher: You may wish to focus in on why the woman seems to be crying. Is she ill? Could this be associated with problems of the aged? Is she lonely?

What items on the T.A.B. will be highlighted?

Picture 2

Picture 2

Note to Teacher: Where are these children going with their parents? The people in this line all seem to be fairly well dressed and yet seem to be very different. Can you speculate about this? If this picture was taken in 1929 or 1930 would these people be pictured the same way?

Select a few items on the T.A.B. as your process objectives for this activity.

Picture 3

Picture 3

Note to Teacher: Possible questions to highlight. *Why are these people smiling? What does wining as noted in this picture signify? Who lost? What was lost?

What items on the T.A.B. are you triggering?

---

*Notice—These are some of the next questions.

Picture 4

Picture 4

Note to Teacher: Some next questions. Who would use a ship like this? Would you take a ship like this for a vacation cruise? Discuss in depth. Use the student responses to stimulate further questions.

What T.A.B. behaviors did you utilize?

Picture 5

*Picture 5

Note to Teacher: The temptation here is to concentrate on the time. Questions such as, what time is it when the big hand is on the nine and the little hand is on the four is typical. There is nothing wrong with this question. Knowledge of specifics is important. However, what else can be asked? Use T.A.B. items #11, #16, #27 to stimulate some next questions.

*Picture courtesy of the Vernor Primary School, Detroit, Michigan.

Picture 6

*Picture 6

Note to Teacher: This picture depicts the workings of a father and daughter. Can you develop a plan or plans that take advantage of this interaction? What questions both cognitive and affective can they be discussing getting ready for Halloween?

---

*Picture donated from the collection of Kristine and Stanley Tracy.

Picture 7

Picture 7

Note to Teacher: What happened? Speculate on why this happened. A discussion of appropriate automobile safety can surely be pursued. Excellent opportunity for creative writing activity using provocative questions as a stimulus for this writing. Asking the next question does trigger the imagination.

Picture 8

Picture 8

Note to Teacher: What makes the hot air balloon rise and continue to fly are appropriate cognitive questions. Why do people enjoy this activity? Do special people enjoy this activity or do special people fly in hot air balloons are appropriate affective questions. The T.A.B., particularly items #34 or #38 may stimulate other provocative ideas.

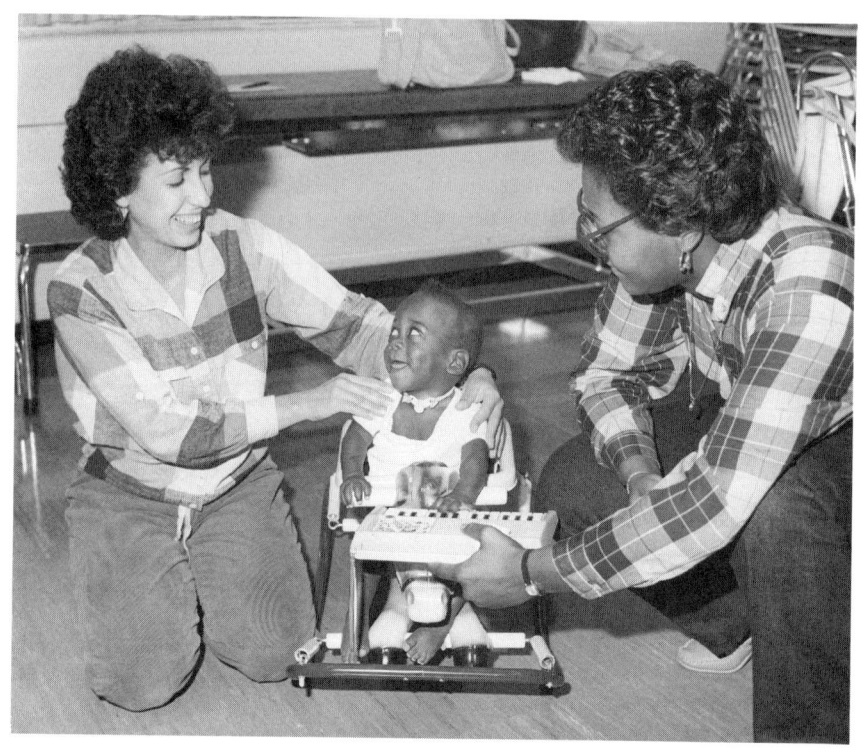

Picture 9

*Picture 9

Note to Teacher: You may wish to create an activity for the parent of this child to use at home during time of interaction. The child may be young, however, the child can listen and from this listening make choices. Parents can be encouraged to ask the next question.

---

*Picture courtesy of *The Detroit Institute for Children.*

Chapter Seven

SUMMARY

It is difficult to summarize ten years of thought into a concise and hopefully meaningful conclusion. So much has been said and written about this topic. And yet, so little has been done. Definitions have been developed for the cognitive as well as psychomotor domains. School curriculums speak to this point quite well. A cursory look at any teacher's lesson plan will give support to the proposition that we tend to be fact or movement oriented. We are constantly asked to list this or recite that in every subject area or course taken at each level of the schooling cycle. It is common knowledge that promotion from level to level is achieved by memorizing certain facts or postulates expected at a grade level or by subject matter specialists. Entrance examinations to colleges, universities and special programs require mastery learning. It is equally an accepted fact that "a sound mind must be contained within a sound body." Therefore programs are available in physical education, dance, movement and for those younger, organized recess. That brings us to where we are.

What cannot be classified as cognitive or psychomotor must therefore be affect. It is out of this ambiguity that some of us have had to work and defend our right to exist. In some circles affect has received a bad reputation. It has meant anything to everything. Handholding, body touching, sensitivity training, confrontation, sharing food, weekend retreats, clarifying values, bull sessions, and show-and-tell are but a few of the activities or handles known as affect. It is not suggested that any of the above activities are inherently good or bad but rather as Fibber Magee's closet, affect contains all things and is therefore all things. Is it any wonder that those who are trainers in affective procedures are usually scrutinized very carefully before permitted in certain school districts or communities? More than one school has purchased one thing and received quite another.

This book is an attempt to bring a definition to this area of concern. Building upon the earlier work of Krathwohl *et al.*, a taxonomy has been developed that attempts to do the following:

1. Provide some objectives that educators may use that are affective in nature.

2. Alleviate some of the pressures that teachers are feeling to create behavioral objectives.

3. Provide a vehicle which will help demonstrate that affectively oriented objectives can be used in developing meaningful teaching and learning experiences.

4. Provide a framework in which to define and classify affective terminology.

It is anticipated that this book will serve at least these functions.

TEACHER FEED-BACK

This author believes that the teacher is in the best position to evaluate his or her performance. After all, the teacher is really the only person who knows what was intended for the activity. An outside observer is handicapped in not knowing the learners or their individual styles; the teacher and his/her individual style and more specifically has little or no knowledge of what transpired in the classroom prior to the specific observation. Teachers have been at a disadvantage here since few instruments are available for them that would permit self assessment. Hopefully, the T.A.B. can help solve this problem. Through the use of audio-tape, video-tape or peer observation, (I hesitate to use the more commonly used term peer evaluation) the teacher is able to identify those objectives triggered on the taxonomy and check this record against the desired outcomes. It is then possible for the teacher to determine rather than speculate about whether or not the objectives were accomplished. A recorded feed-back is more accurate and far more reliable than perceptions. A supervisor friend of mine describes effective teaching as "those behaviors which agree with my biases." The objective for an observed teacher should not be to play to the biases of the supervisor but rather to accomplish important objectives for the learners.

A second consideration in this dimension of teacher feed-back deals with pre-certification programs. Frequently students preparing to become teachers are required to go out into the schools prior to student teaching to observe what learners and teachers do. Since we are all products of the schools it is a safe assumption that we are familiar with teacher practices and school organizations. This assumption is as full of holes as the one which bases teacher tenure on student evaluation. Both assumptions presume that students can evaluate good teaching. Teachers cannot evaluate good teaching. Why do we believe that the untrained can do what the professional cannot do? Affective analysis of any behavior requires a theoretical framework. In other words, you must know what you are looking for and at. Utilizing specific objectives as a basis for the observation directs the viewer to precise acts and deeds. Rather than asking the pre-certification student to "see how the teacher runs her class," we may assign the student the task of determining the frequency of occurrences in which a student or teacher is able to synthesize two or more values into one value. (Item #40.) Not only is this a highly complex activity for a learner, it is highly creative. A discussion regarding what a teacher did to trigger this behavior bears more fruit than one that is generally global and more full of gut level perception than actual happening. Critics of education use this method of global observation to support biases held prior to visiting classrooms. Professionals should be expected to be more knowledgeable and sophisticated in their search for truth.

LEARNER FEED-BACK

Making decisions about what to teach to whom is a tricky business. Even though individualizing instruction seems more a goal than a reality; it is nevertheless what most of us want to see happen. Accomplishing this goal suggests that the teacher have knowledge about the learner, difficult to secure unless the teacher is able to step back and observe the student's learning style. The use of an observational system such as the T.A.B. permits the instructor to focus in on a specific behavior or group of behaviors that will assist her in working with that youngster. The more we know about the learner the more appropriate the instruction.

CURRICULUM DEVELOPMENT

A number of research studies examining classroom interaction point out that the vast majority of class time is spent in attempting to instill bits of information into the student. It has been argued that the aim of third grade is to prepare youngsters for fourth grade. Mastery of subject matter is presumed to be the total expected product and this product will permit the acquisition of more subject matter. Certainly possessing information has its importance, but it strikes this writer that being able to use this information in an intelligent manner is more important than pure memorization. I would hope that knowledge will produce learners who are valuing, feeling individuals capable of making decisions not only vital to themselves, but of value to others.

Chapter Five provided a few examples of how teachers can use their subject matter oriented materials to reach affective as well as cognitive payoffs. It is the judgment of this writer and the belief expressed in this book, that this approach will provide a greater informational feed-back to the learners than the approach most commonly used in today's classrooms. Knowledge for knowledge sake may be useful to pass some examinations or to impress trivia buffs but should not be the foundation upon which all learning is built.

In conclusion, it is hoped that this book will provide to the reader some information not previously available. As teachers become familiar with the objectives described in the T.A.B. they will become easier to use and hopefully important to use. The result may be more competent and more thoughtful curriculum developed by teachers who understand the consequences of their instruction. Using these or any other objectives will not bring a definition to teaching. It will, however, provide a framework around which any dedicated teacher can practice his or her craft. There are other questions to be asked.

Appendix A

TAXONOMY OF AFFECTIVE BEHAVIOR IN THE CLASSROOM

TOT		I		II		III		IV		V		RECEIVING (ATTENDING)
T	P	T	P	T	P	T	P	T	P	T	P	**Awareness**
												1. Listens to others
												2. Receives others as co-workers
												3. Listens to advice
												4. Verbally pays attention to alternative points of view on a given issue
												5. Refers to subgroup(s) (social, intellectual, sex, race, etc.)
												6. Acknowledges some aesthetic factor in the classroom (clothing, furn., design, arrangement, art)
												7. Aware of feelings of others (introvert, extrovert, anxiety, hostility, sensitivity)
												8. Recognizes own bias as a bias
												9. Recognizes other bias as a bias

Willingness to Receive

												10. Seeks agreement from another
												11. Seeks responsibility
												12. Seeks information from another
												13. Pursues another way of doing something
												14. Seeks materials
												15. Asks another to examine aesthetic factor in classroom
												16. Inquires how another feels about event or subject

TOT	I		II		III		IV		V	
T	P	T	P	T	P	T	P	T	P	T	P

RESPONDING

Acquiscence in Responding

						17.	Complies with existing regulations (rules)
						18.	Complies to a suggestion or directive
						19.	Offers materials on request
						20.	Gives opinion when requested
						21.	Responds to a question
						22.	Takes responsibility when offered
						23.	Remains passive when a response is indicated
						24.	Actively rejects direction or suggestion

VALUING

Preference for a Value

						25.	Seeks the value of another
						26.	Defends value of another
						27.	Clearly expresses a value
						28.	Defends own value
						29.	Openly defends the right of another to possess value
						30.	Tries to convince another to accept a value
						31.	Agrees with the value of another
						32.	Disagrees with the value of another

TOT	I		II		III		IV		V	
T	P	T	P	T	P	T	P	T	P	T	P

ORGANIZATION

Conceptualization of a Value

												33. Makes deductions from abstractions
												34. Makes judgments (implies evaluation)
												35. Compares own value to that of another
												36. Attempts to identify the characteristics of a value or value system

Organization of a Value System

												37. Compares and weighs alternatives
												38. Shows relationship of one value to another
												39. Ties a specific value into a system of values
												40. Synthesizes two or more values into one value

CHARACTERIZATION BY A VALUE OR VALUE COMPLEX

Generalized Set

												41. Revises judgments based on evidence
												42. Bases judgments on consideration of more than one proposal
												43. Makes judgments in light of situational context

Characterization

												44. Develops a consistent mode of behavior
												45. Continually re-evaluates own mode of behavior

Appendix B

THE DATE

1. T: "Sandy let me give you a situation to think about for awhile. Suppose your phone rings one night and there is a boy you would really like to go out with on the phone. This is the first time he's called you for a date. He suggests going someplace where your parents have forbidden you to go because they don't like the kind of people who hang out there. What do you tell the boy?" ( )

2. P: "Gee, that's a tough one! ( ) I guess I'd have to tell him that I didn't want to go there, how about someplace else?" ( )

3. P: "If a girl tried to order me around like that, I wouldn't like it too much! I'd have more respect for her if she were honest and said that she wasn't allowed to go there." ( )

4. P: "But wouldn't most girls hate to admit that they weren't allowed to do something? I mean it makes them seem sort of babyish." ( )

5. P: "What if you tell the guy that you're not allowed to go there because your parents won't let you, and he says that you could go anyway—they don't have to find out." ( )

6. T: "What do you think of a person who suggested something like that? Would you girls go along with his suggestion?" ( )

7. P: "First of all, my folks would never forbid me to do anything. They feel that my judgments are pretty sensible and that if I found something objectionable at this place, they know that I would leave. Besides, would a guy calling a girl for a first date be willing to risk not having a date at all? I know a lot of girls would really object to having a guy say that." ( )

8. P: "I agree with Judy. I'm just suggesting, not demanding. If we knew each other better we might be able to talk it all out and reach a decision that way." ( )

9. P: "I think a girl should be able to trust a guy's judgment about where they're going. If a guy knows a girl at all, he should be able to think of something that they could do that they both would enjoy." ( )

10. P: "My folks don't really care about what I do on dates or who I'm with. I'm sort of on my own." ( )

11. P: "My folks bug me left and right—where are you going, who are you going with, what time will you be back?" ( )

12. T: "It sounds as if your parents are concerned about what their son is doing. Doug, I wouldn't want my son out roaming the streets till all hours, not knowing if he's safe or not." ( )

13. P: "But the way they do it—it's such a drag! Don't they have any faith in us? I mean, sure they're interested, but don't they remember how it is to be young?" (   )

14. T: "They probably do. I suspect that's why they're concerned. You know, it's funny, but it's all too true. I can remember when I was your age. I used to gripe all the time the same way you do. But now, with children of my own, I can understand why parents worry about their children." (   )

15. P: "I don't know about the rest of you, but I'd really be worried if my parents didn't show any concern at all. My folks set limits which they think are reasonable for someone my age and they expect me to go along with them. Sure, I could sneak out, or lie about what I'm doing, but I'd really feel guilty. I think I'd try to explain the situation to them; discuss it with them. If I can come up with some good, logical reasons for what I want to do, I'm sure they would be very reasonable about the whole thing." (   )

16. P: "You know, my folks are the same way. I know they want me to have a good time; but they want it to be a safe time. (   ) I know a lot of guys that run around and they don't want anyone to tell them what to do. And it's these same guys that are always getting into trouble." (   )

17. T: "How do you think parents decide what their children should or shouldn't do?" (   )

18. P: "Well, like you said, they remember what they did when they were young. I guess what they want to do is save us the trouble of finding out for ourselves." (   )

19. P: "But shouldn't we be able to find out about life for ourselves? (   ) If they ease the way for us now, what's going to happen after we leave home and we're on our own? Do you think we'll be prepared to meet the problems that we'll be faced with and be able to solve them effectively? I mean you have to start somewhere." (   )

20. T: "Sure, parents want to make things easier for their kids. Most parents I know only want the best for their children. But I do agree, we shouldn't try and do everything for our children. Life is tough enough. I hope we're not producing a generation of kids who are willing to depend upon others for everything." (   )

21. P: "I know that when I get married and have kids, I'm not going to try and run their lives for them. I'll love them and want the best for them, but they have their lives to lead." (   )

22. P: "Sometimes parents get so involved in the lives of their children, they themselves forget that they will have lives to lead after their children have gone. They have to be willing to let go and to let their children lead their own lives." (   ), (   ), (   ), (   )

23. P: "We've sort of gotten away from the original question. We're still faced with what I'm going to tell this guy on the phone. I had something similar happen to me once. I told the guy the truth and we went someplace else. Next morning I read that the place was raided by the cops and a bunch of kids were arrested for drinking while under age. I sure was glad that I wasn't there! The whole incident proved that my parents were right about the kids who hung out there. I learned from that that I could trust their judgment." (   ), (   )

24. P: "If a guy is worth anything at all, he won't condemn a girl for just obeying her parents. Besides, a guy has to look out for his date and he really has no business taking her somewhere where trouble might develop." (   ), (   )

25. T: "It seems as though we basically agree. You think that parents should set reasonable limits for their children; let them lead their own lives with the benefit of the adult's experience; and to use an old cliche—maybe honesty is the best policy." (   ), (   )

Answers to Review Sections

ANSWERS TO QUESTIONS – CHAPTER ONE

1. Skills and/or behaviors that reach above the first level (Receiving) of Bloom's Taxonomy. Those categories that stretch the mind rather than just deal with memory.

2. a. Acquisition of knowledge
   b. Translation
   c. Interpretation
   d. Application
   e. Analysis
   f. Synthesis
   g. Evaluation

3. Reread Chapter One—It's all there—Goldilocks will help.

ANSWERS TO QUESTIONS – CHAPTER TWO

1. a. emotions
   b. values
   c. attitudes
   d. appreciations
   e. desires

   also – impressions
   feelings
   preferences
   interests
   temperament
   integrity
   character
   love of beauty
   aesthetics

2. a. Knowledge based – intellectual skills
   b. See response to question one

3. a. lack of significant research
   b. absence of standard terminology
   c. lack of valid, standardized instruments to assess affect

4. a. Receiving or Attending
   b. Responding
   c. Valuing
   d. Organization
   e. Characterization by a Value or Value Complex

5. a. 3
   b. 4

6. 2

7. 2

8. 4

9. 3

ANSWERS TO QUESTIONS – CHAPTER THREE

1. There is no appropriate answer that can be given here. Hopefully some of the ideas expressed in Chapter 3 stimulated your thinking so that you were able to complete the paragraphs. The fact that you did the assignment is useful in that it should have crystalized some of your thinking in this area.

2. Teachers must possess knowledge and skills about teaching and learning if they are permitted to deal with learners. Just caring (whatever that means) is not enough. Children deserve much more.

3. A. Flanders Interaction Analysis
   B. Bellack's Scale
   C. Medley—Mitzel's "Oscar"
   D. Ryans Characteristics of Teachers
   E. Kaplan's TAB
   F. Simulation

   Of course there are many others that could be listed but because of space were not mentioned in this chapter.

4. If you were unable to respond to this question you will want to reread Chapter 3.

ANSWERS TO QUESTIONS – CHAPTER FOUR

POETRY LESSON – Answer Sheet

1. 1
2. 24, 27, 28, 5
3. 30
4. 27, 28, 5
5. 32, 27
6.
7. 31, 26
8. 25
9. 28, 20
10. 12
11. 1, 21
12. 27, 29
13. 31
14. 21
15. 32
16. 31, 5, 27
17. 20, 27, 28
18. 4
19. 21, 5, 12
20. 12, 5
21. 12
22. 21
23. 30
24. 24
25. 18
26. 14, 13, 8
27. 29
28. 4

ANSWERS TO QUESTIONS – APPENDIX B

THE DATE – Answer Sheet

1. 12
2. 20, 13
3. 27
4. 27
5. 12
6. 12
7. 34
8. 31
9. 27
10. 34
11. 21
12. 31
13. 32
14. 31
15. 26
16. 31, 34
17. 12
18. 21
19. 12, 37
20. 35
21. 27, 39
22. 27, 34, 35, 43
23. 31, 43
24. 27, 34
25. 34, 39

BIBLIOGRAPHY

Bellack, A. A., and Davitz, J. R. *The Language of the Classroom: Meanings Communicated in High School Teaching.* New York: Teachers College, Columbia University, U.S. Office of Education Project No. 1492, 1963.

Berman, Louis M. and Roderick, Jessie A., editors. *Feeling, Valuing, and the Act of Growing: Insights into the Affective.* Washington, D. C.: Association for Supervision and Curriculum Development, 1977 textbook.

Bloom, B. S., *et al. Taxonomy of Education Objectives, Handbook 1: Cognitive Domain.* New York: David McKay, 1956.

Brown, B. B. *The Teacher Practices Observational Record.* (mimeograph) University of Florida, Gainesville, 1966.

Brown, B. B. *The Experimental Mind in Education.* New York: Harper & Row, 1968.

Brown, B. B., Ober, R. L., & Soar, R. S. The Florida Taxonomy of Cognitive Behavior. University of Florida, Gainesville, 1967. (mimeograph)

Childs, John L. *Education and Morals.* New York: Appleton Century-Crofts, 1959.

Combs, A. W. *The Professional Education of Teachers.* Boston: Allyn and Bacon, Inc., 1965.

Flanders, N. *Teacher Influence, Pupil Attitudes and Achievement.* Washington, D. C.: Cooperative Research Monograph No. 12, 1965.

Glasser, W. *Schools Without Failure.* New York: Harper & Row, 1969.

Gordon, I. J. *Studying the Child in School.* New York: John Wiley & Sons, 1966.

Kaplan, L., *et al.* "The Role of College Supervisors of Elementary Student Teaching: Expectations of Student Teachers, Supervising Teachers, and Public School Administrators," *The Journal of Teacher Education.* Vol. XVII, No. 4, Winter, 1966.

Kaplan, L. "Building Observational Systems," *Institute for the Development of Human Resources,* February, 1969.

Kaplan, L. "The Blind Leading the Blind," in the book, *The Assessment Revolution:* New York State Department of Education, February, 1970.

Kaplan, L. "Building Observational Systems," in *SRIS Quarterly,* publication of Phi Delta Kappa's School Research Information Service (now called the Center on Evaluation Development Research), Spring, 1970.

Kohlberg, Lawrence. *Stages of Moral Development as a Basis for Moral Education.* New York: Beck, Crittenden and Sullivan, 1976.

Krathwohl, D. R., et al. *Taxonomy of Educational Objectives Handbook II: Affective Domain.* New York: David McKay, 1964.

Medley, D. M., & Mitzel, H. E. Measuring Classroom Behavior by Systematic Observation. In N. L. Gage (Ed.), *Handbook of Research on Teaching.* American Educational Research Association. Chicago: Rand McNally, 1963.

Merrill, M. D. "Psychomotor Taxonomies," in Singer, R. N. editor. *The Psychomotor Domain: Movement Behaviors.* Philadelphia: Lea and Febiger, 1972.

Ober, R. L., et al. The Development of a Reciprocal Category System for Assessing Teacher-Student Classroom Verbal Interaction. Paper presented at the annual meeting of the American Educational Research Association, Chicago, February, 1968.

Raths, L., Harwin, M., and Simon, S. B. *Values and Teaching.* Columbus, Ohio: Charles E. Merrill, 1966.

Ringness, Thomas A. *The Affective Domain in Education.* Boston: Little Brown and Company, 1975.

Ryans, D. *Characteristics of Teachers.* Washington, D. C.: American Council on Education, 1960.

Skinner, B. F. *Beyond Freedom and Dignity.* New York: Alfred A. Knopf, 1971.

Strom, Robert D. and Torrance, Paul E., editors. *Education for Affective Achievement.* Chicago: Rand McNally and Company, 1973.

Weinstein, Gerald and Fantini, Mario D., editors. *Toward Humanistic Education: A Curriculum of Affect.* New York: Praeger Publishers, 1970.

Woodruff, A. *Basic Concepts of Teaching.* San Francisco: Chandler Publishing Co., 1961.

Films

"Shadows, Shadows Everywhere," A Coronet Film (11 minutes), Chicago, Illinois: Coronet Films.

"Gilly, the Salamander," A Coronet Film (16 minutes), Chicago, Illinois: Coronet Instructional Media.